TIME MANAGEMENT FOR ACADEMIC IMPACT

Academic staff are appointed to teach, research, consult, manage, and learn new technology amidst increasing pressure and dissatisfaction with workloads. They must learn new techniques to engage students who study across different modes, often juggling life and work. This book aims to blend good teaching practice with good time management skills to help academics feel more productive, confident, and in control of their 'teaching side'.

Time Management for Academic Impact explores the relationship between academic workload models, identity, and worldview with our approach to teaching (and research). Using the analogy of life on a treadmill in the midst of tornadoes, it identifies effective, simple, research-informed strategies that will reduce time spent on activities that have low, minimal, or individual impact. Outlining the unique nature of academic work, this book invites the reader to reflect on their own contractual model and helps them to identify 'time thieves', to implement strategies to address these, and to create 'time boundaries' – reclaiming control of their own time. This approach will result in more satisfied students, increased research output, and more time for academics to do the work they want to do.

This book will be of great use to university academics and faculty staff balancing research and teaching loads. It will also help vocational and community college educators and professionals working in part-time, casual, or contract academic roles.

Kate Ames is an award-winning educator, best-selling author, communication professional, manager, wife, mother, student, and part-time military officer. She has spent two decades honing her juggling skills in academic environments with the view that we don't win any marathons if we burn out too early.

TIME MANAGEMENT FOR ACADEMIC IMPACT

Controlling Teaching Treadmills and Tornadoes

Kate Ames

LONDON AND NEW YORK

First published 2020
by Routledge
2 Park Square, Milton Park, Abingdon, Oxon OX14 4RN

and by Routledge
52 Vanderbilt Avenue, New York, NY 10017

Routledge is an imprint of the Taylor & Francis Group, an informa business

© 2020 Kate Ames

The right of Kate Ames to be identified as author of this work has been asserted by her in accordance with sections 77 and 78 of the Copyright, Designs and Patents Act 1988.

All rights reserved. No part of this book may be reprinted or reproduced or utilised in any form or by any electronic, mechanical, or other means, now known or hereafter invented, including photocopying and recording, or in any information storage or retrieval system, without permission in writing from the publishers.

Trademark notice: Product or corporate names may be trademarks or registered trademarks, and are used only for identification and explanation without intent to infringe.

The scenarios in this book are fictitious and included for the purpose of illustrating key issues and ideas. Any resemblance to actual persons, living or dead, or actual events is purely coincidental.

British Library Cataloguing-in-Publication Data
A catalogue record for this book is available from the British Library

Library of Congress Cataloging-in-Publication Data
A catalog record has been requested for this book

ISBN: 978-0-367-40375-1 (hbk)
ISBN: 978-0-367-40377-5 (pbk)
ISBN: 978-0-429-35574-5 (ebk)

Typeset in Interstate
by Apex CoVantage, LLC

Illustration – Simon Kneebone

Dedicated to Jeff and Alan. Early supporters of mine no longer with us. Memories of them are a constant reminder that life is precious and fleeting.

CONTENTS

Preface		ix
Acknowledgements		xiii
1	**Academic life: treadmills and tornadoes**	1
2	**Academic worldviews and justifications**	14
3	**Academic time**	23
4	**What's your time thief?**	35
5	**Controlling the time thief**	60
6	**Inverting the tornado**	75
7	**How do we know it works?**	91
8	**Tornado-proofing for academics**	98
	Index	109

PREFACE

In the beginning

Email from boozy813@gmail.com: Sorry, i couldnt make it to class 2day. I hv questions about the assignment. Can U call me now?

Me: Who are you, what course are you in (I teach into three classes), and what is your best contact? Kind regards, Kate. PS. A polite reminder that I am not your texting buddy, but a communication academic who loves grammar and punctuation because it makes your writing easier to understand. boozy813@gmail.com: Oh, right. Sorry. . . .

I don't deal with too many emails like this anymore, but I used to.

Every hour.

Every day.

My life changed one Monday morning in the early 2000s. Email lists were all the rage. I have always taught classes that include face-to-face and distance education students, and large distance education classes were still unique in higher education at the time. Facebook and Twitter did not yet exist, and learning management systems were very new. We sent study materials by post and communicated via telephone and email lists.

I was the coordinator for two courses in which 1,000 students were enrolled overall. Some students attended on-campus workshops at one of our university's many campuses, but many studied by distance. On this particular morning, I opened my email to several thousand emails (I call this my 'Thousand Email Moment'). Students had erupted about assignment submission requirements over the weekend. As it turned out, there was inconsistency between requirements for on-campus and distance students which technically gave on-campus students an advantage. It was a legitimate issue, but one well and truly out of my scope of control.

Even 20 years later, I can still recall that feeling of panic that morning. My hands went numb, my head exploded, and I felt the sense of my eyeballs being pushed out the front of my skull.

I turned off the computer and sought solace in one of my colleagues over coffee to calm down, not returning to my desk until lunchtime. When I did, I worked progressively

x *Preface*

to respond to the issue, but it was too late. The beginnings of 'complaint cancer' had taken hold (you will learn more about this if you read on). My term, and relationship with students, never really recovered from that point.

I resolved, in that moment, that things would be different.

The problem was that I didn't know how to make things change.

I was still a 'newbie' (see Chapter 1). I was entirely focused on my teaching because it was always right in front of me. Up until that point, I hadn't had a real reason to change my practice. It seemed quite legitimate that *all* of my time was student-focused during term.

Everyone had email lists. We were expected to be available to students in class, by email, and by discussion forum. We were still grappling with the way communication technologies were changing the face of teaching. As we put our slides online, students didn't need to come to class. Students like 'boozy813' could simply email us to ask what they had missed. Organised students would do the work for students who didn't need to get organised, because they could simply ask a question on a forum and the organised student would respond.

Metric-based evaluations started to increase the level of pressure. If we didn't respond, a student could complain, our teaching evaluations would suffer, and we would feel the consequences. Our contracts might not be renewed, we might not get the promotion we wanted, we might not get the courses we wanted to teach. Few people I worked with challenged the system or practice. Everyone worked long hours, as did I. Everyone responded immediately to students to prevent the email wildfire. Or they didn't, and students simply complained or contacted those who did.

Over the past couple of decades (roughly), I have worked to refine my practice. I have been very lucky. As tenured faculty (or a permanent academic), I have had the room to try and test a few strategies without risk of my contract not being renewed. I have balanced research, teaching, and management loads, and juggled life working full-time with family (I had two children while completing my PhD) and a long-term part-time military career (I deployed twice on short-term assignments while completing my PhD - which took eight years to finish). I don't consider myself a star. I have been rejected for grant applications, teaching awards, journal publications, and promotions.

We are very lucky to now have an amazing array of resources available if we want to be better PhD students, teachers, and researchers. This book, however, was born out of my frustration that most academic texts explore 'organisation' with a focus on increasing our writing or research productivity. As an example, I have learned a huge amount from Maria Gardiner and Hugh Kearns, who run the organisation Thinkwell. Maria taught me to not feel guilty about juggling lots of different things at once, and the importance of keeping planes in the air by paying attention to them but then focusing on one when it needed to land. I attribute this guidance to being able to research as a manager and teaching scholar.

I'll list more resources at the end of the book, but I have always sensed a gap in how we teach more efficiently and effectively within an academic environment as a complement to our research. I meet so many academics who don't like their teaching, are

Preface xi

frustrated, or see it as an interruption to what they want to be doing. I used to be the same. This is compounded by pressure to adapt to online teaching, which we now know takes more time and effort to do well.

We need to shift our thinking given that teaching takes up so much of our time. It's all very well if we write for the first hours of every day, or get up before the kids to write, but if we've set six pieces of assessment for the term, allow students to email us outside of contact hours, and don't have scheduled appointments for postgraduate students so they can insert themselves into our thinking at any point in the day, we're still going to be working at 10 p.m. every night.

This book is a collection of practices, reflections, and knowledge refined over many years, and shared locally with others. It is a response to the suggestion given to me on more than one occasion: 'You should write a book about this stuff!'.

This is not intended to be a 'time management' book, as such. It's about reflecting on how you become more efficient and effective as a teacher so you can do more of what you love, whatever that may be.

ACKNOWLEDGEMENTS

It is impossible to succeed in academic life without a strong support network, professionally and personally. Our life is public – we lecture in front of classes, give conference presentations, write publications – and we, more than most, must learn to cope with critique. It's the nature of ideas and research. Without support, we cannot flourish.

There are, in so many years, too many people to mention individually, so I will acknowledge the general community of amazing peers, academic and professional, at Central Queensland University Australia, and my amazing colleagues in the Australian Defence Force. All of you help me be better at what I do.

To my broader circle of colleagues within the academic community in Australia and internationally, thank you also. The incredible network we can now access daily, thanks to social media, has been liberating. I value your diversity. We are all so incredibly different, but are able and willing to share similar stories about juggling work and life. My 10 minutes a day on Twitter often make my day.

I do need to pay a special tribute to my mentor and friend Professor Jacqui Ewart, from whom I learned much of what I know and who has been the most generous of colleagues. I will never forget the days of helping you manually cross-check grades belonging to thousands of students against an Excel spreadsheet to make sure there were no calculation mistakes in the days before such a thing as a learning management system existed. You helped me get started and remain my constant 'rock'.

To my #academicpets Hunter, Scarlett, and Hamish, thanks for keeping me and my keyboard company in those quiet writing hours along the way.

To my extended family, husband Jason and children Maeve and Joshua, thank you for keeping me grounded and making sure I remember what's most important every day.

The final acknowledgement must go to the amazing students who cross my path. You come from all walks of life, and challenge, frustrate, and inspire me. Every day I get to share the classroom with them is a day I learn something new, and for that, I am thankful.

1 Academic life

Treadmills and tornadoes

It's very easy, in the face of mounting stress and tension, to view an academic career from a deficit position. It's quite difficult to find public discourse that is positive about academic life. That is, we focus on all the things that are wrong with it.

But we know that many of us choose academic life because of what it can offer. Flexibility, social advocacy, pushing the limits of knowledge, generating new ideas, and autonomy, as examples. We might not be the best-paid bunch of workers in the world, and we may be working in an increasingly commercialised, metrics-based environment, but there's a lot to like about what we do.

We help build generations of future practitioners, thinkers, and scholars. Many of us really love our jobs. It's why we find it so hard to switch off and why we respond to the 'boozy813s' I referred to in the preface via email late in the evening.

There's a lot of research on the current 'state' of academia. I cover some of this in the next section in detail, but it can be depressing. Academic work is predicated on service – the idea that we will give some of our work for free. We do this in the form of service to journals, to community, to organisations (including our own), and to students. Within that context, we must still provide feedback for 120 essays in ten days while teaching four on-campus classes per week, organise a field trip, submit a research proposal, and prepare a course outline for next term. And that's if we're working full-time. If we're working casually, there's always that work we must do for which we don't get paid: student contact out of hours, orientation to materials, extra reading to keep on top of the discipline or teaching requirements, travel, etc. The list is long. And then there's the unpaid research work we might do as casual researchers, such as fieldwork and article writing, to secure a tenured position.

We can see how easy it is to become resentful of expectations. We might have flexible work hours, but the work still must get done.

The approach promoted in this book is not about being perfect or having everything we signed up to do delivered on time, every time. In fact, we may find we are suddenly late for things because we aren't breaking ourselves as we try to meet unreasonable self-inflicted deadlines. We should question who we are as scholars, and our views on teaching, research, and service. We will establish a baseline from which we can engage in some of the strategies discussed in the book. Anyone open to self-reflection and asking

2 Academic life

hard questions about why we do something (like answer a student email at 4 a.m. or mid-afternoon on a Sunday) can make great progress in clawing some life back.

As you read, question your practice with an aim to restore balance to your life. Become comfortable with the reality that there will never be enough time that you will always be expected to do more than you physically can, and that you will always be compared to others who have different lives and manage things differently. Goalposts will always change, and it is likely that in the course of an academic career, you will get rejected for promotion/tenure/grant because 'you haven't got enough of X', even though you were told that's what you needed to increase in your portfolio when you specifically asked: 'What do I need to increase in my portfolio?'

You may not have a lot of control, but you can have some.

What we know about academic life

If you are feeling like you are drowning in work, that you are always at the beck and call of your students, that you have too many supervisors to whom you must answer, that the goalposts keep changing, you are not alone. The tertiary sector internationally has become more complex, and demands on academic staff have increased. It is an international problem, and the trend has been evident for some time. The education sector at all levels works under financial pressure, has to be responsible to government if publicly funded, and is increasingly competitive and responsive to a wide range of metrics.

Internationally, we have seen a push toward formalisation of qualifications for teaching staff. The suggestion that teaching faculty need a formal teaching qualification in addition to discipline-based qualifications is contentious – for many, it's just another thing to do. New academics, often appointed just on the cusp of completion of a PhD, can be under the greatest pressure. Just as they are trying to mine their thesis to generate publications and engage with opportunities associated with grants or projects open only to early-career researchers, they are suddenly required to complete a qualification in learning and teaching.

There are a few specific reasons for feeling the pressure at an individual level. The two I will focus on are academic workloads and academic identity. Understanding both are foundational to the premise of this book.

Workload

The first point of pressure relates to workload allocation, and expectations associated with individual academic profiles; that is, what you're expected to do as a research scholar, as a teaching scholar, or anywhere in between.

Attempts to develop a system-based workload allocation in universities and colleges have developed into a fine art, and many continue to find the perfect approach. One identified problem is that workload allocation models are often related only to teaching, which is easier to measure. In some institutions, research is not included in workload allocations at all (Wolf, 2010). This means we must find time outside allocated (and remunerated) hours to complete research tasks.

If research is included in workloads, the time allocation is inconsistent with performance measures that enable tenure or promotion. That 'one day per week' is not going to be enough to support publishing six papers per year, as an example. The 3 hours per week you have allocated to run a class doesn't reflect the real time taken up by miscellaneous student contact, administration, and preparation.

Indeed, it is telling that when we search for the job profile of an academic in the UK, we find the following statement when it comes to working hours:

> Working hours are 35 hours per week. However, you may need to work extra hours in order to fit in time for lectures, tutorials, your own research and administrative tasks. Some lectures and seminars take place in the evening.
>
> Part-time contracts are available for lecturers. It's also possible to take a career break, but you'll need to maintain an active research profile. Some lecturers take a sabbatical (usually up to one academic year) to concentrate on their research activities in greater depth.
>
> (Job Profile, higher education lecturer)

It is interesting to reflect on how little has changed in a few decades. In 2000, Craig Mcinnis noted the following trends in his research into academic work:

- Most academics have an interest in teaching *and* research.
- The number of academics with a preference for research increased during the 1990s.
- Overall satisfaction with the job has decreased.
- More than half of academics say their work is a source of considerable stress.
- Average working hours are around 50 hours per week.
- The amount of time spent on teaching has declined.
- Class time accounts for most of the hours during any week.
- Pastoral care requirements have increased.
- Learning new technologies, or creating course materials for students, has had a major impact on work time.

(Mcinnis, 2000, p. 144-145)

At the time, reasons cited by academics for hindering good teaching practice were, in order of greatest hindrance to least: too wide a range of students' abilities, too many students, lack of up-to-date equipment/technology, current research commitments, and having to teach subjects outside your area of expertise (Mcinnis, 2000, p. 147).

If this sounds familiar, it is. Little has changed (Dobele, Rundle-Thiele, Kopanidis, & Steel, 2010; Stensaker, 2018), but since the early 2000s, we have been further impacted by developments in technology that extend the classroom beyond four walls.

Some interesting points noted in Mcinnis' research at the time were that you were more likely to have more time allocated for research and thesis supervision at a

4   *Academic life*

sandstone/older university, and expected to have more hours allocated to teaching in a newer institution (2000, p. 148). You were more likely to be required to teach outside your area of expertise and hampered to achieve research outcomes if you were a newer academic, and less likely to be required to teach outside your area of expertise or hindered by research commitments if you were a late-career academic (Mcinnis, 2000, p. 148). Not surprisingly, professors were those least likely to be hindered in their teaching. The hierarchy in academia was very real.

There is little evidence if any that this has changed. It's relevant because there is a good chance that you are reading this book because you are either new faculty teaching at a university or college, or you are more experienced but feeling completely overwhelmed. If you are a new academic in a new university, you are not only more likely to be teaching in areas that are not your specific area of expertise, you are also likely to be dealing with other challenges, such as heavier student loads and greater diversity in student skill and knowledge – described as 'too wide range of abilities' by Mcinnis (2000, p. 149). If you are teaching at a university that prides itself on providing access to education for students, it is probable that your students may need more support in basic areas such as literacy and critical thinking.

Thus, the reason to feel under pressure and a reminder that you're not alone.

Academic identity

The second reason for feeling the pressure of academic life at an individual level relates to academic identity. We choose academic life for a range of reasons. Some become hooked as an undergraduate student in a research course, proceed to Honours then PhD, work in a research centre, and only know a research/academic environment. At the other end, some come from a professional background, and start their career employed in part-time teaching roles within a discipline. They decide they like the teaching, so pursue a teaching career within a university or college.

There are many other entry paths, but in my experience, these two extremes are the most common and represent some of the greatest challenges. There seems to be a constant binary tension. On the one hand, we have staff who have only ever worked within an academic environment which is more flexible than most. They are used to the paperwork, the grant and teaching cycles, and the way research teams operate. On the other, we have staff who are used to being organised, focused, and oriented to 'doing' rather than thinking.

The diverse range of categories of employment for academic staff in the sector is staggering. We can be employed as any one of multiple options from tenured research-only to contracted or casual-teaching or research-only staff. We could be a postdoctoral fellow, funded by a grant, who needs to find time to submit further grants to fund our research/career. We could be a PhD student trying to find time to conduct research while also accepting teaching contracts to support our lifestyle. We could be a teaching-based academic who spends most of our time during the day in class with students or interacting with our teaching team.

We receive lots of advice about how to write and research as an academic – 'write often', snack write, write in the morning when your ideas are fresh. No matter what strategy we have in place for our research, however, *we will always experience 'teaching seep' if we don't become better at organising our teaching.*

This doesn't just mean getting better at writing 'to do' lists, or prioritising our time or projects so we get the most important things done first. In my experience, that just adds to stress as my 'to do list' continues to grow.

For some, a completely different way of thinking about our relationship with our work, our students, and assessment is required. Some of us may be addicted to being busy, or so busy we can't see a way out of our current practice. Many of you reading this book will be in the middle of the teaching 'fight', so will find it difficult to think about all of this with a sense of freshness.

We'll come to strategies later, but first, I would like you to reflect on your own personality and your relationship to students, assessment, and teaching.

Being a 'teacher'

We make a lot of fun of 'types of teachers'. Public discourse is full of categorisations. Indeed, I will add to this shortly. We know that a teacher's personality is important – in fact, it's argued that it is the most 'complex variable in the educational process' (Göncz, 2017, pp. 75-76). We know that attitude toward academic life impacts on the way we approach our tasks (Flecknoe et al., 2017; Rosewell & Ashwin, 2018). Overall, however, there is limited empirical research on the relationship between teacher personality and approach to workload. In my experience as a mentor, however, I believe personality plays an initial role. When I say initial, it's because this is what we default to in the absence of guidance. It's what comes naturally to us – we teach the way we were taught ourselves, or in reaction to the way we were taught. This, I think, also rings true for those who have been taught how to teach.

However, there are some people for whom I can offer no words of wisdom. That's because their worldview is so set, or they have a deep-seated need for power, love, or control that they have no wish to change (even if they think they do). I am not a psychologist and don't pretend to be, but I have come up with a range of 'types' I encounter when I mentor academic staff. This should be taken with a sense of fun, while also feeling a bit 'close to the bone'. While I use these categories loosely and in that light-hearted sense, I do in fact call on them when I make decisions about who I am going to work with and how I am going to work with them.

The newbie

A new academic faces many issues. If we have been appointed without a PhD, then we will usually be hired conditionally (meaning we are under pressure to complete our PhD as a condition of appointment). We are overwhelmed with new administration systems, and often don't have control of the course we are teaching, as we will be appointed to

6   *Academic life*

teach courses that are coordinated by others. We are keen to learn, but often commence without guidance or supervision if our senior academics are distracted by grants or their teaching load. Bad habits can be learned early.

Issues: Some newbies have a strong personal agenda – complete the PhD, do a specific type of research – and are resistant or resentful of the teaching that has been allocated to us as a condition of our appointment. We see it as something we 'have' to do.

The counter-newbie

Counter-newbies are those who have been around forever. We are often in positions of influence, such as teaching committees, and have very firm views of how things need to be/are done. We are genuinely busy, but are often caught up in operational matters and can sometimes revert to 'easy' rather than 'important' when making decisions. Counter-newbies have strong institutional networks, have a genuine commitment to service and helping our work colleagues.

Issues: Supervisors who are 'counter-newbies' can be resistant to change and too busy to supervise a newbie. If we do supervise, we may be over-directive in our approach. Counter-newbies may seek advice, but are prone to reject this quickly. We may, therefore, not be a target audience for this book because of our resistance to new ideas.

The ambi (ambivalent)

The ambi is someone who is 'cruising' as a tenured academic. Often mid-career, we have reached our self-directed peak. We like our job, we like our students, we don't take on extra work, we don't do too much service. We accept that teaching is part of our lot, but we also do a little bit of research in an area that interests us. We are quite self-contained and generally fly under the radar.

Issues: Because ambies are quite happy with our lot, we may not empathise with others who are new or struggling, or ambitious. We don't really need the information in this book, because we aren't juggling as many balls as others and have made the most of the flexibility that comes with a tenured academic life. Many aspire to be an ambi. We are, however, increasingly rare in academia as pressure increases for research or teaching outcomes.

The research purist

Research purists have entered academic life to follow our research passion. We may not like to teach, or if we do, make sure all our teaching is contained into a single term, so we have most of the year to focus on our research. We may be resentful of the time that teaching takes away from conducting research. Our research is a priority, and it can take us days (or weeks) to respond to students. We can get away with this because we receive large grants, spend time building research networks, and actively publish. We are interested in supervising research of higher degree students.

Academic life   7

Issues: Research purists, despite not wanting to or liking teaching, are often excellent teachers because we are so knowledgeable and passionate about our area of interest. This book may be of use to research purists because it provides tips to help 'contain' teaching time so that we can have more time for our research.

The teacher

Teachers fall into two possible categories – we either focus on teaching because we love it, or we focus on teaching because it's busy, but is easier than doing research. Teachers make ourselves openly available to students, and spend hours on refining our teaching materials. Teaching academics may default to a love of teaching because it is more instantly rewarding. We love to see 'lightbulbs' go on in class. We are often good at what we do, and don't see possible co-dependence with our students as problematic.

Issues: Like social media, teachers can get addicted to evidence of personal influence. We can become dependent on instant feedback to feel satisfied at work. The issue for the teacher is that we feel we can't disengage from students. Some don't want to, but others don't know how to create the space we need to pursue other projects. Many teaching-focused academics lack confidence in conducting our own research. We default to teaching because it's important and keeps us busy. The issue is that when it comes to promotion or increasing salary, teaching academics look one-dimensional and lack the breadth of experience needed for many positions.

The project-focused academic

Some academics want to pursue only one interest. We want to finish our PhD if we are lucky enough to be appointed without a PhD (which is increasingly rare) or work on a specific research project. Project-focused academics are difficult to spot at recruitment, so may be appointed as permanent faculty. A project-focused faculty member may not be the best team member and is particularly focused on single ideas or areas of interest. We generally don't volunteer or engage with others, and are excellent at protecting our time.

Issue: While project-focused academics are excellent time managers, we are so at the expense of other things that will make us a better academic in the long term. There may come a point where others will be reluctant to work with us, and we may find it difficult when getting to higher levels to juggle the multiple balls that come with managing a department or larger scholarship/development project.

The prepper

Preppers are academics who are currently completely overloaded because we are preparing to step to the next level – promotion, tenure, incremental review. We usually need to demonstrate that we have been working at the level above into which we are seeking promotion. This means we will take on more service, more grants, more teaching – all

8   *Academic life*

at more complex levels – to tick the boxes we need to tick. We become quite overloaded as we chase a dangling carrot, or the potential of 'being ready' for that permanent job when it comes.

Issue: Overwork for preppers can become quite extreme. The key issue is that getting promoted as an academic is extremely difficult – we are measured against what we haven't achieved as opposed to what we have, and that list can be *very* long (not quite enough publications, not quite enough research, not quite high enough satisfaction rates in our teaching). If we are waiting for that full-time or permanent fractional job to come up, we are quite literally waiting to find that needle in a haystack. We may feel like we are chasing an endless tail, and without an excellent mentor and clear guidelines, preppers can 'lose our lives' for long periods while getting ourselves into what car racing enthusiasts would describe as the 'pole position'.

The professional casual

Universities are successful on the back of professional casuals. Tutors, markers, reviewers – a group of people referred to as 'sessional staff' make the world a bit more seamless for permanent faculty. Professional casuals come in a range of forms. We may be retired full-time staff who are topping up our incomes in pre-retirement mode, professionals who are wanting to enhance our CVs, or PhD students topping up scholarships or earning money to support our study. Professional casuals can work across multiple courses at the same university, or for many universities in the same term. The term 'professional' is very apt here – professional casuals are often highly organised, able to work across a range of topics, and have our own systems to ensure we remain on top of everything. Some professional casuals are quite happy to work on an 'ebb and flow' basis, but others are waiting for the opportunity to become tenured staff.

Issues: Professional casuals are attractive for universities to hire because of the simplicity of our contracts. We are hired for very specific teaching/research purposes. If we are a professional casual, it is possible that we are trying to progress our academic career 'between' paid hours and therefore are at risk of being underpaid and overworked.

The rollercoaster

Most of us will fall into the rollercoaster category. We enjoy our jobs and the opportunity to teach, research, and provide service. We sometimes thrive on the adrenaline that comes with pressure of a deadline that we're keen to meet – an award or grant application, an abstract for an overseas conference that we would *love* to attend. We do, however, get overwhelmed at moments that seem to come as a surprise when they shouldn't. These moments include grant application deadlines that happen at the same time each year and drive us underground for weeks (such as Australian Research Council deadlines in January each year, or National Institute of Health Research deadlines in April and May in the UK); marking blocks that we should have planned for because we

Academic life 9

set the deadlines for the assessment; and class preparation for term, even though we have taught the same course every year for the past decade.

Issue: The key issue for those of us who are rollercoasters is that we don't have space to think. Once that rollercoaster leaves the point of departure, we're off and we can't stop. Every hour is filled with research, teaching, student contact, and school meetings, with some hours feeling more out of control or grinding upwards than others. We feel continually guilty that we aren't doing more because that colleague in the next office is writing more papers, getting promoted, being successful in grant applications.

Why does all this matter?

Some of you may recognise yourselves in the described groupings, while others might be arguing vehemently with me, with 'What would she know?' being the loudest voice yelling inside your head. The purpose of this chapter is to help you realise you are not alone. If you recognise even a bit of yourself or others you know in these categories, you can know that issues that come with teaching at university level tend to be universal.

Now you know you are not alone, we can talk about academic life from the perspective of 'treadmills and tornadoes'.

Academic life: tornadoes and treadmills

A day as an academic can feel like a day of running on a treadmill while dodging a tornado (if you are not already trapped in one). Our workloads feel like they are out of control, and we feel like we have limited touchdown. We spin around and around at the top, touch down for a short period and then spin off again. At the same time, we are trying to run on a treadmill, subject to due dates of term commencement and completion, grant submissions, reporting, and examination periods. If we don't pay attention or stop, we fall off the back and then must run twice as hard to catch up. It's exhausting. Even if we are lucky enough to get a semester off or have some time out, we then have to jump back onto a moving treadmill that continued on without us.

Academic environments will always be 'treadmill and tornado' country. I will unpack these concepts in specific detail in later chapters, but the trick is to become expert at the treadmill workout. This means we should be able to hop on and off the sides of a moving treadmill with skill and precision, and learn to invert the tornado.

Why treadmill?

Universities and colleges are institutions that have been here generally well before we turned up and will be here (hopefully) long after we leave. In this respect, they have similarities with churches, government, and the military. They usually have deep roots in communities. Older universities may have been the genesis for a town, but newer universities have often been raised by or advocated for by a local

10 *Academic life*

community. Online universities that have a global reach are built on systems rather than by communities, but support the development of strong and enduring virtual networks.

In all cases, our presence as a staff member in a university in whatever form will be ultimately fleeting. We will make our contribution to our students' growth, our research may make a contribution to a body of knowledge, but the very nature of the academy is that our ideas will be challenged, debated, and perhaps relegated to a zero citation count if they weren't considered worthy of engagement by anyone. Ultimately, our students will go forth to shine in their own way, perhaps (I think hopefully) brighter than we have.

We may spend all our time devoted to the service of the university and our students, and some of us do come very close to being irreplaceable due to our unique knowledge base. Overall, however, the institutions we work for are far bigger than we are as individuals.

When we start academic work, we are therefore inserted onto a treadmill already in motion. This treadmill has been going for years – in some cases, centuries. There's always a forthcoming teaching period or block, materials needing to be prepared, rooms needing to be booked, guest lectures needing to be organised, tutors needing to be oriented to what the teaching term will bring, and students needing to be inducted.

If we are lucky, we have been appointed for a particular purpose and given time to 'gather ourselves' before the onslaught of a teaching term. If so, we have the opportunity to carefully step onto the treadmill and start at a slow speed. This is rare in my experience, and can come with its own monumental workload expectations, such as writing a completely new set of courses in a short period of time.

Most of us get inserted onto the treadmill while it's at some form of speed. We're handed materials, class lists, and timetables, and told to simply 'go forth and do'. If you are reading this, you're possibly already on the treadmill, preparing for term while juggling fieldwork, writing papers, and managing research students. Once we're on, it becomes difficult to stop, slow, or get off.

If you are required to start on a treadmill at speed, it's easy to understand that you may develop bad habits early without the opportunity to change direction or rethink your practice. When I commenced working as an academic I didn't expect that we would work in such strict cycles – teaching terms, course materials, timetabling, marking, examination preparation, and grading. My first couple of years were spent in a state of constant disbelief that it was 'this time of year/term/week' again. I became more adept at managing everything as I became used to the cycles, and implemented the strategies in this book. I still fall off the back of the treadmill occasionally, but mostly, I'm work-fit enough to manage at a steady state.

We must remember that the academic treadmill will *never stop*. Ever.

Terms will come, students will enrol, the next call for papers will appear in your inbox. If you catch me in the first week of term, I will *always* look just that little bit shell-shocked. But only for 1-2 hours. I have learned to manage the treadmill, as, hopefully, will you.

Academic life 11

Why tornado?

The term 'tornado' refers to the relationship between effort and impact. A normal tornado relies on 'topspin' to generate effect. The topspin is necessary for momentum – without spin, we don't move forward. However, impact is random and we sometimes have no idea where a tornado's funnel is going to land (if it does), or how many people it might affect.

For some, having a positive impact on one individual student can be enough. We may hear (or say): 'If I can make a difference to just one student, it will have been worth it'. The problem with this is that the effort, which is spin, often comes at our personal and professional expense. The preparation we do for an on-campus lecture to which only three people turn up, or that scenario we develop that becomes dated straight away, or that research we do for a term's worth of material that suddenly becomes irrelevant because of a development in our profession (such as a new software) – all of this is topspin with minimum impact (or touchdown). There's a sense that all that effort amounted to not very much.

I refer to *minimum impact* as something that doesn't last or impact more than one or two students. This is 'tornado-type' work. Examples of 'tornado-type' work might include:

- doing 8 hours of preparation for a one-hour lecture that will only be current for a specific term;
- responding to 25 student questions on the same topic over a few weeks;
- writing examination questions that will only get used once and can't be re-purposed;
- giving a lecture on a case study that is current only for a specific date and not captured to be used again as an ongoing resource; or
- setting a fantastic assessment piece that tests a piece of software but becomes updated or outdated during or immediately after term.

We end up spinning because we're on the treadmill, with limited time to think about working smarter. We are always going to need to prepare a good lecture, but how do we maximise the impact so that the effort we put in is worth it? Can we use the lecture, or the information we included in it, again? Can we turn our research for class into research for publication? How do we future-proof our course content?

The busier I became in my career, the more I questioned tornado-type practice. I sought answers to these questions, and learned the importance of investments of 'pre-emptive' time, such as a half-hour block of focused thinking. I have always maintained a teaching load, even in administrative roles. It became particularly important to think about effectiveness as aligned with efficiency.

I therefore began to focus on 'inverting the tornado'; that is, spinning less but covering more ground on impact. This was easier to conceptualise than do. In some cases, it required pushing back on institutional policies, and in all cases, it required me to evaluate

12   *Academic life*

my practice holistically. I have had to reconsider my worldview and challenge strong and long-held beliefs about teaching, relationships, power, and expertise.

Our next chapter will focus on the link between these long-held views and teaching efficacy and time.

Chapter 1 summary and activities

This chapter has provided an overview of academic life that should feel familiar to anyone reading this book. It included some categories for self-identification to reinforce that we're not alone, and introduced the concept of treadmills and tornadoes as a way to conceptualise workload and flow.

Reflective practice often starts with recording thoughts and reflections. I recommend a teaching journal or a blog. When you do manage to control your teaching and start to enjoy it, you should find that your results improve. Recording your reflections progressively becomes incredibly useful, particularly if you want to apply for teaching awards which always benefit from a baseline analysis. For example: '*I used to do (insert your former practice). I realised that the consequences were (insert consequences). I reflected and discovered (insert details of what you found). I applied (insert strategies) to improve my practice. The results were (insert results). This benefited students by (insert details of benefits)*'.

These suggested activities are prompts. We may come back to them as we progress through this book.

Chapter 1 activity 1 - *what do you like the most about academic life?*

As a start, complete this sentence:

   '*I love being involved in academic life because . . .*'

We hear a lot about what's wrong with academic life. Indeed, we touched on issues in this chapter. Focusing on a positive may reinforce why you're reading this book and trying to improve things as a reminder when the going gets tough.

Chapter 1 activity 2 - *which category?*

While the categories in this chapter are intended to represent faculty in a light-hearted way, it's highly possible that you may have seen yourself reflected in the options. If so, which one and why? What resonated, if anything? Where there any that were missed?

References and further reading

Dobele, A., Rundle-Thiele, S., Kopanidis, F., & Steel, M. (2010). All things being equal: Observing Australian individual academic workloads. *Journal of Higher Education Policy and Management*, *32*(3), 225-237. doi:10.1080/13600801003743323

Flecknoe, S. J., Choate, J. K., Davis, E. A., Hodgson, Y. M., Johanesen, P. A., Macaulay, J. O., . . . Rayner, G. M. (2017). Redefining academic identity in an evolving higher education landscape. *Journal of University Teaching & Learning Practice, 14*(2).

Göncz, L. (2017). Teacher personality: A review of psychological research and guidelines for a more comprehensive theory in educational psychology. *Open Review of Educational Research, 4*(1), 75–95. doi:10.1080/23265507.2017.1339572

Job Profile, Higher education lecturer. Retrieved from www.prospects.ac.uk/job-profiles/higher-education-lecturer

Mcinnis, C. (2000). Changing academic work roles: The everyday realities challenging quality in teaching. *Quality in Higher Education, 6*(2), 143–152. doi:10.1080/713692738

Rosewell, K., & Ashwin, P. (2018). Academics' perceptions of what it means to be an academic. *Studies in Higher Education*, 1–11. doi:10.1080/03075079.2018.1499717

Stensaker, B. (2018). Academic development as cultural work: Responding to the organizational complexity of modern higher education institutions. *International Journal for Academic Development, 23*(4), 274–285. doi:10.1080/1360144x.2017.1366322

Wolf, A. (2010). Orientations to academic workloads at department level. *Educational Management Administration & Leadership, 38*(2), 246–262. doi:10.1177/1741143209356362

You can check out some reading on different types of teachers if you're interested – some are more light-hearted than others.

- BoredTeachers.com refers to the 14 types at www.boredteachers.com/humor/species-of-teachers-youre-sure-to-find-in-any-school
- Unicheck refers to 17 types of teachers at https://unicheck.com/blog/types-of-teachers. Gojimo has only five types. Some try to put a bit more science into it. For example: edustaff links teaching types to the Myer-Briggs personality type indicator: www.edustaff.co.uk/blog/80_
- Göncz (2017) reflected on the 'Five Factor Model', which is worth reviewing for a more academic approach to the topic of teacher personality.

2 Academic worldviews and justifications

Academic journeys are individual. We take different paths, influenced by different contexts and circumstances. Most of us, however, will teach students at some point. We might teach the way we were taught, or have firm views on how students learn based on our own learning style. We may not be willing to try new things because we find a 'groove' that works. We may use textbooks as the basis of our teaching content (indeed, we may have written the textbook), we may like essays because they are easy, and a 1-hour lecture/2-hour tutorial schedule has worked for the past 20 years, so why change now?

Once we're on a treadmill and have found a rhythm that works for us, we can find it difficult to motivate ourselves to try new approaches. In addition to personal experience, our approach to 'everything teaching' – including writing lectures, designing assessment, engaging with students – is informed by our view about knowledge, or worldview. Many things influence worldview generally, but this chapter focuses on personal worldviews and explores preferences for research and teaching, and some common justifications for resisting change.

Carving out time for research and writing is well covered in a lot of writing about academic life. It is widely acknowledged that those of us who can carve out that time in our day are more productive and ultimately 'successful'. Containing the 'other stuff' related to teaching practice is not. To progress, we must be prepared to recognise our context and motivations, and challenge our thinking.

Personal worldviews

'Interpretivist' or 'positivist'

Most academics would be familiar with the terms 'interpretivist' and 'positivist'. Academics in the humanities would be more likely to work from an interpretivist perspective, whereby there is no such thing as a concrete right or wrong, and the world can be viewed from a range of perspectives and interpretations. Methods of teaching and research can be adapted to the question at hand. Those working in *stem* fields (science, technology, engineering, and mathematics), however, might be more likely to view the

Academic worldviews and justifications 15

world through a positivist lens. There are concrete answers to questions, and methods of teaching and research need to be fixed to yield these correct answers.

This is very simplistic. I'm not suggesting that all *stem* academics are fixed in their thinking or approach, or all humanities academics are fluid and adaptive. Indeed, some of the most creative people I know work in engineering and science, and some of the most fixed people I know work in history and literature. The point here is that if you have firm beliefs about how knowledge is gained and expressed, then you may have greater difficulty adopting a student-centred approach to learning. You may believe that students can't be experts, and that letting them set agendas in the classroom is irresponsible. Certainly, it may be potentially dangerous to let first-year students take control in a science or engineering lab (but maybe not). You may be someone who needs to see concrete evidence that a new approach will work before you are willing to try something, or you may be willing to be an early adopter. Whether you are fixed or flexible will affect how willing you are to try new things or engage with new practices.

Provide support vs foster independence?

How we respond to students may be based on how we view them and their need for support. Stories of students receiving absolutely no response from academic staff are quite common. On the one hand, we have students who are ignored, and on the other, we have students who receive an instant email response at 10 p.m.

Our approach to our relationship with students may be pragmatic, or may be attributed to our worldview. For example, if we are a research academic who is interested mainly in postgraduate students and spends much of our time in the field or in labs, we may see our undergraduate students as irritants or those we *have* to deal with. We may like them, but may be resentful of their intrusion into our space. We delegate our junior staff or tutors to deal with these students, or just ignore them. Our approach to these students is informed by the worldview that: '*I do not need to respond to my undergraduate students immediately (or at all) because my research is more important than them*'.

A senior professor or tenured research academic may be able to get away with this, but anyone working as a research-oriented academic on contract may find that this lack of attention to any teaching side has longer-term consequences if they are not successful in attracting future grants. Many academics do not get tenure or achieve promotion if they do not have the teaching side in hand.

Alternatively, we may be a teaching academic who feels chained to our desk ready to respond to students. The idea that a student would wait for more than an hour is an anathema to us. We believe that our role as a teacher is to support students. Our worldview may be: '*I need to respond to students because it is easier to just answer their question now. Otherwise they will have more questions*'. We may not explicitly believe this, but what we are really saying is: '*My students' experience and supporting them is more important than my research/scholarship*'.

16 *Academic worldviews and justifications*

Education as a privilege or a right?

Many academics lament the decreasing standard of students as universities corporatise, or increase the diversity of entry pathways. More students than ever are entering universities and colleges internationally, and a greater number of pathways to higher education have increased the diversity in our classrooms. This presents challenges to teaching academics. Students with poor literacy, critical thinking, or comprehension skills may require extra time and effort as we try to explain difficult concepts. This is exacerbated if a student's first language is different than our own.

We could argue against this, and for higher standards of entry. This would make our lives easier. If we feel this way, then we may believe that education is a right, but we are supporting the view that education is a privilege and should be restricted to those who deserve it. Our mental talk may sound a little like this: '*I wish they would stop letting these students in. They can't write properly, can't read, and it's unlikely that they will succeed*'.

However, there is now so much evidence that supports the premise that disadvantage breeds disadvantage, and that education is an enabler to opportunity that maintaining this view is increasingly unsustainable. The alternative view might look like this: '*It can be really hard to teach given that we have an open entry policy to our college. But students have a right to the best possible education. I may make it easier for everyone if I develop my materials and assessment with the student who will struggle the most in mind*'.

Teaching-focused institutions have a routinely higher failure rate than older institutions with higher entry scores due to a more 'open door policy'. For example, in one institution an overall failure rate might be 25% as opposed to 12-15% in another institution with a more competitive entry requirement. We could see this as a failure rate, or a pass rate. My own worldview would see this as a pass rate – more students who would otherwise not had the opportunity to study passed their courses.

The way we think about our students, and the challenges associated with teaching to an increasingly diverse student body, reflects our worldview and therefore impacts on the way with which we engage students.

Organisational culture and systems

There is an ongoing tension between research and teaching, and the way in which either is preferenced at our institutions impacts on our worldview (or at least the view we are willing to express publicly). If I had a dollar for every time I have been told to buy out my teaching as a priority when working with research grants, I would be a rich woman. People are surprised when I talk about how much I love teaching. I do. It's genuine, and it's personal. Research is a bit of a game, pitching ideas to people who may or may not give us money depending on what is on an organisation's or government's agenda at any one time. However, teaching is between me and my teaching team and students. It's scary, immediate, hard, frustrating, challenging – all at once. It always feels like stepping

Academic worldviews and justifications 17

off a cliff – you never quite know what will happen. Research for me feels a bit steadier. While results might be unexpected, which is always exciting, good research is methodical and there's a sameness that comes with each project.

So, to honour the magnet on my fridge that states: 'Do one thing every day that scares you', I remain a teaching academic. I retain a teaching and supervision load, despite now working in management. It's important to me that I remain at the coalface. I still have a central role in communicating with my students and developing and reviewing assessment. My general rule is that I would rather pay for a great research assistant than buy out my face-to-face teaching.

Everyone's going to be different on this, and that's fine. Talking about research or teaching in this book in the way that I am going to runs the risk of playing into a very simplistic view of academic life, which has been challenged by those studying the complexity of academic work.

The dichotomy between research and teaching is systemic. The orientation toward research or teaching is something that academics raise, as illustrated by the extensive comments on Tanya Golash-Boza's blog post 'What's the matter with a forty-hour week for academics?' (2012), and more broadly in research into academic identity (see Clegg, 2008). Regardless, most staff working in a higher education setting will be required to fit some form of research, engagement, or service into their workload.

Broader organisational systems, policies, and processes can also influence culture.

As an example, I assess teaching award applications at my institution. When I commenced, I noticed that we received applications that referred to responding to student's emails within 24 hours of receiving them as an example of good teaching practice. Accessibility to teaching staff is one thing – accessibility to teaching staff 24/7 is another. I argued that responding quickly to student emails isn't a necessary marker of good practice; indeed, it may mask poor practice: _'If I respond quickly to emails, then students won't complain about the lack of clarity in the assessment question'_, as an example. The committee agreed with me, noting that I had been the first to raise this specifically. We discussed the wording of criteria, so that it would remove the encouragement to work above and beyond normal hours to be considered good teachers. Applicants are now explicitly advised that responding instantly to students is no longer an example they can cite as good practice.

This is an example of institutional response and amending culture. It levelled the playing field. Some of us, I argued, weren't able to work on weekends and respond instantly to students. We shouldn't be disadvantaged or be considered poorer teachers if we had different life circumstances.

Feeling needed or important

Academic life is something many of us fight very hard for. It's a profession that values hierarchy for good reason. Where middle managers can be targeted in organisational restructures as younger employees with new ideas represent greater value for a company, the value for universities and colleges is knowledge – built by research, and

18 *Academic worldviews and justifications*

disseminated via teaching. Someone who has achieved the level of professor can't be replaced easily – the thousands of hours of research, the walking library/database that person carries around inside their head, the stakeholder contacts, the understanding of implications of research methodology, the most effective teaching methods – all of this is acquired between 15 and 40 years of work.

One of the unfortunate byproducts of this hierarchy is academic arrogance. It's a relatively well-recognised phenomenon within 'the academy'. Australian academic Dr Inger Mewburn dedicated a specific post on her Thesis Whisperer blog to this very topic, 'Academic Arrogance' (2012), when she referred to arrogance as being the dark side of knowledge. Inger generously reflected on a scenario in which she realised that she was guilty herself of demonstrating arrogance to a student. I too have been guilty of this early in my career. Inger is a well-known mentor of postgraduate research students in Australia with a large following on social media, having built her exposure through her popular blog. Mewburn has written widely on academic life more broadly, and refers to teaching at university as 'Academic Hunger Games'.

There seems to be an acceptance of academic arrogance. It feels normal to feel that we are going into potential combat every time we engage in public discussion, either in person or in writing. This arrogance might come from a range of bases, but it seems worse in those who had to fight hardest for their position. There's a sense that 'it was tough for me, so it needs to be tough for you, too'. I have seen PhD students who were the first in their family to get a university degree, let alone a doctorate, graduate and immediately demonstrate evidence that they think they are better than others. Having a title 'Dr'/'Professor' means something very deep and genuine – it becomes their identity, so any challenge to status or title is taken personally, and any opportunity to demonstrate that they have the knowledge behind the title is taken.

Again, this is related to worldview. I don't think I'm smarter than anyone because I have a PhD. I perhaps work harder and am more persistent than others, but the reason I have a doctorate is that I generally finish what I start. Sheer determination to finish what I started got me a PhD. I was also pragmatic – I wanted to teach at university, and I needed a doctorate to be able to do this without feeling like I was an imposter. Overall, I have been lucky. I come from a very middle-class background with every opportunity afforded. I never felt like I had anything to prove, aside from being female, which has had its challenges over the years. The only time I have felt the need to yell about my achievements was after I failed a promotion round. I decided to list every one of my awards and significant achievements at the end of my email signature just to remind myself that they weren't a dream. Once I was over the hurt of rejection, I returned to my normal email signature, but I do remember being surprised at the number of people who seemed to notice that list!

We can assume, therefore, that status is important as a general comment within the academic community. It explains why we take our profession so personally. Through our study, we have invested time and money into our career, but find it at the mercy of metrics and many factors beyond our immediate control.

Common justifications

When I work with peers, common justifications emerge as we reflect on the relationship between work habits and time management.

The most common excuse I hear is quite simply: 'I don't have time'. Many of us don't (initially) feel we have the space for deep and focused work, or any time we do have left should be retained for research or the work we want to do. We don't care that much about teaching. The idea of stepping back and making change to established practice is too high risk because we have a constant sense of overload. It's just easier to keep going, even knowing the negative impact this might have. It's a bit like being on a diet or a budget. You know what you need to do, but there's always a reason why you can't start today.

The justifications I sense and see, however, are:

- fear;
- lack of control; and
- lack of confidence or knowledge.

Fear

If we have never tried something new, and work in an environment where our performance is routinely measured against metrics such as student satisfaction, our likelihood of embracing change is limited. I often meet peers curious about my strategies, but reluctant to try them in their courses. It's simply easier to stay in the middle lane and keep going as always. I have also worked with those who have tried something different, and failed, only to be very reluctant to try again. Interestingly, I always think this is a great point to start from for documenting our reflective practice if we haven't already. A *failure-to-success* narrative has great potential when applying for teaching awards.

Lack of control

Lack of control over workload – or more directly, being bullied into working on a task in a particular way – is also a reason some people cite for not changing practice. This is reflected to me in the form of comments such as: *'I can't do it because I'm not allowed to make changes'* or *'I don't want to make changes. It will make my life too difficult'*.

This might be understandable in the case where one academic is filling in for another for a term. The academic on leave doesn't want to come back to a completely different approach to his or her course. In other cases, however, a head of curriculum or discipline may have very firm views about assessment, content delivery, office hours, lectures, and so on. This makes it very difficult for individuals working within a course environment to adjust curriculum or approach that may affect workload. As an example, a school or course team might pride itself on its face-to-face teaching, and two-hour lectures are the normal standard. This is despite the fact that only 20 students are enrolled in the

20   *Academic worldviews and justifications*

course, and of these, only five turn up to class. Preparing a two-hour lecture for five students and then dealing with those 'What did we miss?' questions is an example of wasted time. Alternatively, academics may be required to set examinations as assessment because the course is externally accredited, and the accrediting body requirement includes examination.

Lack of confidence

Finally, some academics believe that they are not knowledgeable enough about the course they are teaching to adjust. This is somewhat of an elephant in the room, because technically, certainly in Australia, our requirements are that academic teaching staff are qualified to teach the courses into which they coordinate or teach. The reality, however, is that new staff are often asked to teach courses that sit at the edge of their knowledge. We might be a film studies major asked to teach into an introduction to communication course, an environmental scientist asked to teach into a sociology course, or a human resources academic asked to teach into an introductory management course. While we may have touched on the core skills required to teach into these courses because we covered them ourselves in our undergraduate degree, we are not expert in teaching introductory level students and need to spend time to refresh our knowledge. It's stressful for us, and possibly an issue for students. To survive, we simply teach what's on the curriculum without really engaging in the topic, or we must spend copious hours reading into the course so we can teach it.

Taking stock

We are often not compelled to truly reflect on what we're doing unless we reach a crunch point. This might be when applying for a new job, seeking tenure or promotion, or simply seeking a full-time or fractional contract as opposed to a casual hours-per-week contract. It's a competitive environment – our resume will be reviewed against others with similar experience and background. Our mid-ranging student satisfaction rates, which aren't spectacular in either a good or bad way, may be the difference when being compared to someone who has an excellent teaching record with similar publication output.

All of this is important because it's going to influence the way you approach the rest of this book. If you are guilty of having demonstrated arrogance, then there's a chance that your behaviour has at times generated student complaints. If you have a positivist worldview that holds you to creating content for your students and testing them on their ability to recall that content, then there is a chance you're on a treadmill of content updates, examination writing, examination marking, and reviews of grades.

There is a very strong correlation between deep and focused thinking and personal reward for academics. The more we can research, publish, create excellent teaching materials, the more power we ultimately gain over our career. We get promoted in various ways, and have more say in the type of research, teaching, and service we do.

Fear, lack of control, and lack of confidence or knowledge will affect how willing we are to examine our practice. We may need to engage a mentor early, or work on the assumption that we can find a mentor or get support in some way as we review and refine our approach.

Linking worldview and attitude to time

Worldview and time are directly linked.

For example, if we're a firm positivist who works in a research-focused institution, believes that students must earn their way into university by achieving a very high standard at school, and are the first in family PhD who genuinely believes we're more important and deserving than others, there's a good chance we're not going to change our practice. Our research track record is our focus, we don't respond to students, we don't pay a huge amount of attention to our teaching, and we're protected by an elitist culture within our organisation. We're also required to set exams, so don't need to change the way we assess students. We are used to the 'education for the masses' approach.

It may appear on the surface that there is no need for change. To change requires effort and effort requires an investment in time and knowledge. By the end of this book, however, it should be clear that effort can result in greater efficiency and effectiveness. This change may also require an adjustment in worldview. The following activities will ask you to think about yours.

Chapter 2 summary and activities

This chapter has introduced some of the influencing factors in the way we approach our academic work, particularly teaching. It highlights the very personal and complex relationship many of us have with our work, and others we work with. Its purpose is to establish our baseline views before we start to make changes in our practice which will positively affect our time and effectiveness.

Chapter 2 activity 1 - which worldview?

Reflecting on your worldview at the very beginning of your journey creates the foundation from which you can then progress. It's like working through your attitude toward money and spending before you start to work on a budget. It can be very confronting.

Reflect on your worldview.

- Did you find anything in common with those we covered in this chapter?
- Are you willing to change or adapt your views? If so, what will you need to do in order to change your practice?

Record your responses to these questions in general terms. You may reflect on this later, when we ask you to apply the most appropriate strategies to help you transition to new approaches.

22 *Academic worldviews and justifications*

Chapter 2 activity 2 – which excuse?

If you are reading this book, you have already recognised there's a problem or room for improvement in your life. Reflect on which excuse comes to mind when you think about changing your practice.

Which of the following best applies to you?

1 *'I don't have time, but know I need to make changes if I want to get some life back'.*
2 *'I am scared of making change because I'm worried. I am comfortable with my current practice, even though I know there is room for improvement'.*
3 *'I am too stressed out to even think about this. I just want to get to the next chapter'.*
4 *'I have no control over my practice as I am told what to do by my peers or superiors'.*

If you answered (1), your task is to create space. We'll have strategies for you later in this book.

If you answered (2), you need to build your confidence and make incremental, rather than drastic, changes. I'm a fan of this anyway. You will find that strategies suggested at the end of this book are based on the 'small steps' approach.

If you answered (3), you just need to keep reading!

Finally, if you answered (4), hopefully you will find there are some strategies in this book that will help you 'control what you can control'.

References and further reading

Clegg, S. (2008). Academic identities under threat? *British Educational Research Journal, 34*(3), 329–345. doi:10.1080/01411920701532269

Golash-Boza, T. (2012). *What's the matter with a forty-hour work week for academics?* Retrieved from http://getalifephd.blogspot.com/2012/03/whats-matter-with-forty-hour-work-week.html

Mewburn, I. (2012). *Academic arrogance.* Retrieved from https://thesiswhisperer.com/2012/08/16/academic-arrogance/

For further reading on some perspectives on academic work, read:

Rosewell, K., & Ashwin, P. (2018). Academics' perceptions of what it means to be an academic. *Studies in Higher Education*, 1–11. doi:10.1080/03075079.2018.1499717

3 Academic time

I asked you to consider your views and your approach to work in the last chapter because how we think about ourselves and our work influences how we allocate our time and our views on 'work-life balance', if there is such a thing. This chapter explores perspectives on academic time, time from a budgeting perspective, the '9-to-5' question, work seep, calculating hours, and working with a fixed schedule.

Academic time

Time is power. We know complexities exist in the relationship between time, power, and academic flexibility. Some scholars perceive they have no problem with work-life balance because they love their work so much. However, this can manifest in higher levels of 'volunteerism', because people are prepared to work long, unpaid hours. Indeed, there is a strong argument that the appointment, tenure, and promotion system is predicated on a culture of volunteerism. This is particularly obvious when it comes to research, which we are generally expected to do in our own time if we want to reach levels required for tenure and progression.

We don't usually quantify our time. We're not encouraged to, because the figures are scary when we map out required hours against what is humanly possible.

As an example, administrators may complain that academic staff aren't attending meetings during a teaching break week. However, behind the scenes, those academics will be working to grade 120 essays so that they may be returned to students within 10 working days. These essays are expected to take 30 minutes each to mark. This, in pure mathematical terms, would account for a minimum of 60 hours of marking during a two-week period. Throw in having to convene some workshops, moderate assessment, communicate with tutors, respond to students, and battle technology. The list of possible jobs to complete in addition to marking in that fortnight is long. The mere act of accessing a learning management system and downloading or opening a paper can take valuable time.

We can see that the numbers start to stack up quickly, and sometimes impossibly.

We'll talk about the impact of technology later, but the aim at this point is to encourage you to think about the reality and cost of time. How much time do tasks that routinely sit on your 'to do' list really take, and what is the cost and value associated with those tasks?

24 *Academic time*

Time as a budget

Time is quite concrete, like money. Once spent, we can't get it back. In simple terms, we want to save time so we can free ourselves to do work we want to do within the range of allocated work hours for which we are paid.

Thinking of time in budgeting terms requires us to consider fixed and variable time costs. Fixed costs are those things that can't or won't change. Variable costs are those things over which we have greater control.

In academic life, fixed costs might be:

- scheduled lectures, workshops, laboratory work, tutorials;
- stakeholder meetings that are contractually required;
- faculty/school meetings; and/or
- research activities identified in a budget, such as focus groups, field trips, interviews, and observation periods.

These fixed costs are scheduled activities that we must include within our weekly routine. Just how fixed these costs are depends on where we sit within the 'academic food chain'. If we manage a project or are a senior academic, then we may have more say in timetabling, contractual agreements, or how we design our research. If we're new to academic life, then we will have (or feel we have) limited ability to change what seems quite fixed. If we don't turn up or complete these activities, there may be serious consequences unless we have a legitimate reason, such as illness.

There are different views on what costs are fixed and variable. Variable costs are those which are necessary, but we can work to make a difference in their overall total, like groceries in a family budget. We can reduce variable costs if we make deliberate decisions to ensure we reduce waste. In our case, we are also seeking to maximise effect – happier and more successful students equate to a happier and more productive us. Variable costs include:

- marking;
- student consultation periods;
- writing and scholarship; and/or
- peer mentoring and support.

Variable costs are those which can easily blow out, and they are those which are ultimately those we have more control to contain.

Like any budgeting process, identifying what we spend our time on from a fixed and variable perspective can be confronting. Examining variable time costs also requires us to place a value on our time if we want to make cuts to or amend how we spend it.

When you work through your schedule later in this chapter, I'll ask you to think of it as a budget – spend only what you (technically) have, and try to find ways to save. You won't be able to buy more time, but you may create more value in an hour.

Work seep

The likelihood of work 'seeping' into our non-working lives is high if we don't have set working hours, and there is an expectation that we will be motivated enough to conduct research and scholarship in our own time.

Seep is defined generally as something that may flow or leak through porous material or holes. Some aspects of work seep are accepted as natural for academic life. These periods are when the treadmill is running at its fastest, whereby our workloads increase monumentally for blocks of time. These include marking periods, or administration to set up courses for the term or year.

If we don't contain work seep on a routine basis, however, we remain in a constant state of being alert – to student and supervisor requests, stakeholder issues, issues with lab management, as examples. In the longer term, this isn't good for us, even if we love our job and feel happy to volunteer our time, all the time.

The '9-to-5' life for academics

Life as an academic is not '9-to-5' for most of us. It can be for much of our year, but there will be periods when it is not possible to work standard hours, or when working to another schedule is the only way we can be more productive. Life will happen. We can usually adjust – the flexibility academic life can afford us is one of its well-known attractions.

I am not an advocate for the premise that an ideal academic day should be contained to '9-to-5'. This simply, I think, misrepresents the reality of academic life. It doesn't allow for the ebbs and flows of term (requiring those 60 hours of marking outside standard hours) and 'life happens' periods, such as raising children or caring for elderly parents. It also doesn't account for teaching across time zones or night classes, doing research at night or on weekends (such as community-based focus groups, running a sleep lab, conducting fieldwork in the evenings) and grading papers.

Flexible hours within academia suit institutions because if the span of hours was more fixed, the costs of teaching delivery would be astronomical. In the current system, we can be asked to teach at night without being paid overtime or compensation. The idea is that we balance our hours – if we are working at night, or 70 hours per week during a teaching term, we would be, on principle, expected to take some hours off when it's quiet.

The reality, however, is that many of us don't do this.

I thought I did – until I tracked my hours for a year. I did so because I was feeling guilty about taking a few mornings off to catch up on life. As a former editor who had worked standard '9-to-5' hours, I didn't feel comfortable about taking time off during the week, despite having spent an entire weekend marking and taking online lectures at night.

I decided to keep an accurate diary of what times I really worked. This was a worthwhile exercise.

26 *Academic time*

It turns out I had worked my entire yearly quota of hours by September. I technically worked the final three months of the year for free.

I didn't feel so guilty after conducting that exercise. I now build compensatory activities into my schedule. If I work a late night, then I'll have the following morning off. Some people will fill this space with more work – that's fine if it's what you really want to be doing.

In tracking my hours, I didn't examine specifically what I was doing with them. I was simply tracking my 'time spending'. That helped me feel less guilty and take a few mornings off during term after a night class, but didn't help me work smarter. I just felt better about the flexibility I had.

Creating structure within flexibility

How do you create a schedule when you have maximum flexibility in how you spend your day, driven primarily by the need to be responsive to students and fitting in some research when you can?

In his book on productivity, *Deep Work*, author Cal Newport (2016) talks about that moment he realised the discussion between what and how – he knew what he had to do, but not how to do it. I also knew that I needed to manage my time better, but didn't know how. I read widely. I became bitter and cynical quickly. General time management and efficiency strategies just never seemed to fit. I became firmly convinced that a lot of the proponents of schedules didn't have children or caring responsibilities, or had support at home or in the office.

For example, if I had a dollar for every article that advised me to get up early, I would be wealthy. However, I have been effectively single for more than a decade in the mornings as my husband has always left the house at 4:30 a.m. This means that I manage two children on my own – first before day care when they were little, and then before school (I have always worked full-time). It didn't seem to matter how quietly I tried to get up and move around; one would always wake and require attention.

I tried strategies like working in bed (I would routinely fall back to sleep quickly), and oiling door hinges (which worked until another noise was made). I have one particularly light sleeper who 'wakes when the sparrow breaks wind'. Simply turning the kettle on, starting the computer (I tried leaving it on), tapping on the keyboard – the list goes on – would prompt two little feet to hit the carpet, come directly to me, rub her eyes, and say: 'I'm hungry'.

I gave up. By setting unrealistic expectations, I became too stressed too quickly and didn't pay my children enough attention. This is also in the context that I have always owned a small farm, so also needed to feed horses and sheep in the mornings. Between tears (mine and the children's), baas, and neighs, I was a total wreck by 7 a.m.

I have therefore worked in the evenings to compensate for later starts and early finishes a few days a week. It's not that I am working evenings to fit more work in – it's that I am working evenings to complete the required work that allows me to do other stuff. This evening work has included holding online classes for distance students, marking, and student office hours.

Academic time 27

I have tried many different strategies. I tried the sign off schedule at the end of day to create a boundary between work and home promulgated by Cal Newport in *Deep Work*. I found that due to my life circumstance (kids), and because I had a more flexible job than my partner, I was routinely called to pick up sick children when they were little. It felt like I was leaving work early to collect a child every second day. Needing to leave work suddenly meant I never got the routine down pat. I adopted a strategy learned during a workshop with Thinkwell's Maria Gardiner (n.d.), who advocates for a 'park on a hill' approach. If I needed to leave work suddenly, I quickly wrote down a 'TO DO' note - one action that would get me quickly started the next morning or time I looked at that task.

Ultimately, I learned to apply a range of techniques that I was able to use as needed. The point here is that life and schedules will change, but our overall ability to fit what we need to into the hours we have won't. It's what we do within these hours that is important.

How many hours?

My schedule is based on a 40–45-hour week. It's more than I am technically paid for, but reasonable for my level. I had never really thought specifically about hours associated with categories of academic work until I was selected for a competitive early career researcher programme. Those selected to participate were under significant pressure to produce research outcomes.

At the time, I was a balanced academic who resisted the pressure to outsource all my teaching. I loved teaching, and didn't want to pay someone else to engage with my students. I did, however, want to conduct research or inform my practice with discipline-based scholarship. My worldview was that I couldn't teach well without being an active researcher in media - a discipline that was rapidly changing.

When trying to work out how I would complete the requirements that seemed acceptable (I had promised to submit six research papers in one calendar year), I realised that I needed to think about schedule. I had previously relied on summer breaks to catch up, and had published at the rate of one or two papers per year for some time (quite a reasonable rate, I now accept). To complete six papers, which I was told was possible and certainly seemed to be what was normal for some of our research staff, I needed to take a different approach.

It became immediately clear that I was not going to be able to catch up in my semester break. Our institution teaches three 12-week terms. I teach from March to October (Terms 1 and 2) and have usually had my 'break' in third term, meaning 12 weeks of non-contact with students between October and March. We are entitled to six weeks of holiday leave (we're very lucky), including a Christmas break. At the time of this programme, I was taking most of my entitled leave in late December and January to coincide with Australian school holidays. I am also a military reservist. As a result, I receive another four weeks of defence leave as one of my conditions of employment (again, very lucky). So, out of the 12 weeks that I don't teach, I'm supposed to be on leave for 10 weeks of that period.

28   *Academic time*

I immediately recognised that if I wait for a 'break', I have only two weeks to complete research requirements consistent with a balanced profile.

It was never going to happen. I was a busy teacher, coordinating up to five courses over two terms (one of which was a first-year undergraduate course with 200–300 students), managing industry placements, and supervising research higher degree (RhD) students.

Somewhat unbelievably now, I had never previously confronted the reality those figures presented to me. I had simply battled on and tried to catch up when I could.

It became immediately apparent that to achieve the milestones for that one year as a member of the programme, I needed to maintain a consistent approach *throughout* the year rather than rely on a catchup period. I needed to build research into my weekly routine for that year while on the programme.

I was aware of the promoted practice to 'write for the first few hours of the day', but with such a large teaching load consistently, I found I was suffering from 'teaching seep'. I could write for a couple of hours in the morning, but the teaching-related work of marking didn't go away. I would work into the late hours on the evening to ensure I wasn't becoming a heat-seeking missile target for students. This meant I was pumping out the publications, but was completely exhausted from juggling everything.

Calculating hours

Academics generally do not have standard working hours – these are averaged over a year. At the time, the annual number of hours for an academic at my institution was 1,730. Once my personal leave entitlements were deducted (10 weeks), I knew I needed to be able to all my work in 42 weeks (if we assume that I am going to take all my leave) but fitting 1,730 hours into 42 weeks penalised me for leave periods and required me to work 41 hours per week. I decided to calculate the actual breakdown for a week based on a normal leave profile (4 weeks of leave) and arrived at 36 hours per week.

1,730/48 weeks = 36 hours

As a balanced academic at the time, my percentage workload allocation was 40/40/20. That meant 40% of my time should be research, 40% should be teaching, and 20% should be service related.

Weekly, therefore, the breakdown at the time was:

Research (40%)	Teaching (40%)	Service (20%)	Total
14.4 hours	14.4 hours	7.2 hours	36 hours

Prior to this calculation, I had dedicated Thursdays to write my papers. Looking at these numbers made it immediately apparent that this wasn't going to work – one day only gave me 8 hours. Nor was changing my schedule to starting my day with 2 hours of

Academic time 29

research before everything else (which would amount to 10 hours over a 5-day block). How could I balance this out?

I worked on my schedule so that I started each day with 2 hours of writing/research/ scholarship. That meant that I achieved 10 hours or writing/research. I needed to find another 4 hours, which became Thursday mornings. Overall, I was able to maintain a routine of 14 hours per week.

Once that was sorted, the question then became: How do I contain my teaching hours within 15 hours per week? Research can be contained generally – hours in labs, hours in library, hours conducting focus groups/interviews/fieldwork. It's quite quantifiable. For me, it was the teaching effort that bled into my evenings and weekends.

Teaching, while also quantifiable, can explode. Reviews of grades because a student didn't understand feedback, re-marking assignments, and examining plagiarism cases. I always refer to term as diving into a deep blue sea – you go down and don't come up for air for 12–16 weeks.

Every institution will have different approaches to how they require teaching staff to calculate workload, and as previously discussed, some people will have more flexibility than others.

In my case, I am personally responsible for 120 students per term, generally. Because we receive a workload that recognises the managerial load for coordinating a multi-campus, distance education course, I do receive teaching buyout for some of my classes. I therefore manage all the distance education students (approximately 90). I run online lectures for them, develop all teaching materials, and mark all their work. I sometimes coordinate a team of markers at five campuses around Australia. I also recruit markers, orient them, liaise with them, and moderate their marking.

My father used to complain that during term, I was impossible to catch during work hours. I explained to him that during a marking block, which lasted a couple of weeks, half an hour of talking to people was half an hour I wasn't marking. I generally turned my phone off when marking or grading papers, and turned it back on often when it was too late to return calls.

As noted in a previous chapter, marking students comes with a concrete load. Marking 120 first-year students will usually take 30 minutes each essay (that's 60 hours). I am required to complete marking within 10 working days of receiving the assignments. I therefore need to find 30 hours per week to complete this task. If I keep researching, I need to add 14.2 hours, which takes that figure to close to 45 hours per week. Add service and class requirements – up to 8 hours per week – and we're looking at a 53-hour week. That's before I've even touched emails.

We can see, therefore, that during marking periods, long hours are going to be par for the course. Many of us drop our research during these periods, but this results in losing momentum and taking too long to get back into the research swing.

Once I transitioned to being a teaching scholar, after much soul-searching about where I saw my career heading, I had to revisit these hours. My percentage of time allocation became 60/20/20. In this case, my one day (Thursday) would have been enough for research but the teaching load and number of students impacted on my ability to set aside one full day.

30 *Academic time*

My hour breakdown became:

Research (20%)	Teaching (60%)	Service (20%)	Total
7.2 hours	21.6 hours	7.2 hours	36 hours

Only 22 hours a week to cover a teaching load doesn't seem like enough. But over 5 days, it's almost 5 productive hours per day. Seven hours of scholarship or research per week amounts to roughly 80 minutes per day (give or take). Service, or those things we do for others such as counselling students, volunteering, mentoring, membership of committees, contribution to the organisation (however your organisation may define it), then accounts for 80 minutes per day.

I am conscious that in this model, I'm working at slightly more than 40 hours per week, but not much. I cut this back by a few hours – say 20 hours for teaching (4 hours per day during a normal week), 60 minutes per day for research and scholarship, and 60 minutes per day to ensure I get lunch and incorporate a few breaks. This is more realistic and accounts for interruptions. It also aligns with the now fairly well-established premise that we have a limit to how productive we can be.

When I first identified my daily or weekly requirement, I was unsure of how to make weekly, rather than block, attention to tasks work. It was completely different than the way I had worked, whereby I had tried to quarantine one day per week for research. I was always resentful – that day, Thursday, seemed to always be the day people I needed to talk to wanted to talk to me. I was *always* being interrupted on that day, or important meetings I was required to attend were scheduled. I rarely made great progress on the papers, writing, or reading I needed to do. But I needed to – not necessarily for promotion or tenure, but for my personal satisfaction. Even as a teaching scholar, I am committed to scholarship and I love the process of research and reflection.

Making fixed hours work

Once I worked out what my weekly hours were *supposed to be*, I created a timetable. I decided that it was more efficient and effective to teach my online students at night. I held online lectures on Monday evenings, and virtual office hours on Wednesday evenings. This suited my life when my children were smaller because they would be asleep when I went back to work between 8 and 11 p.m. I took up a jewellery class on Tuesday mornings to compensate for my late Monday evenings. I always felt a bit guilty when driving to class, but as soon as I was at my studio table, I was engrossed in metalsmithing for a few hours until lunchtime.

The timetable, incorporating fixed hours, has proved flexible. I have become 'one of those' early birds who works for an hour or so in the morning now that my children are older and sleep longer. I do maintain standard working hours now that I am in a managerial role, although I generally log off around 4:30 p.m., which gives me a few hours in the afternoon with the kids, logging back on for an hour at night. I still try to fit my work associated with management and teaching into 25 hours per week. I have a vastly

Academic time   31

reduced teaching load, taking a small online-only writing or speech class each term with up to 60 students. Scholarship remains a vital part of my practice. At the time of writing, I supervise RhD students, including six PhDs, and one Masters by research, and am a member of a number of funded research projects.

My practice works for me. All schedules are completely individual. In the activities section of this chapter, I will ask you to examine your available hours and complete a possible schedule for yourselves. We will come back to this as we work through issues and strategies.

This book targets the teaching side of academic work. Everyone will have different requirements in terms of teaching load and associated workload allocations, and any figures mentioned here are illustrative only – you'll get the chance at the end of this chapter to work these out for yourselves. All of this is also written in the absolute knowledge that things are not as straightforward if you are appointed on a contract or to a position that has a percentage allocation of an overall workload (for example, part-time at 60%).

A word on level playing fields

Academia is not a level playing field. Promotion criteria are considered 'opaque' (see Sang et al., 2015, p. 243). Any accounting for career interruptions that should be applied often aren't, and there is a very clear link between numbers of papers/grants/income/RhD completions and promotion. Activities that have more intangible outcomes, such as implementing a mentoring scheme that changed culture in a department, don't count. It's brutal.

The most common metrics include publications, impact factors, and research income. If we are a teaching academic, we may be a slave to teaching evaluations which ask students how satisfied they are with our teaching or the quality of the course. Regardless of how theoretically and pragmatically flawed the approach to these evaluation or success metrics might be, they are very real for us as we attempt to identify what is required to be 'successful'. There are many factors at play.

In a system whereby metrics and numbers are linked with 'success', there appear to be three types of people who 'succeed':

1   Those people who have more time or happily work longer hours.
2   Those people who feel they must work longer hours to get ahead.
3   Those people who are more efficient with the time they have.

It's possible that we could be 'those people' in points 1 and 2, but we want to work on being the person in point 3. But we don't just want to be more efficient – we want to be more *effective*.

> ***Illustrative example:*** *One Monday morning, I overheard a student conversation outside my office whereby two students were complaining about a lecturer who had not responded to an assessment-based question that had been posted to a discussion forum over the weekend. The assignment these students were discussing had been due that morning.*

32 *Academic time*

> *The students were indignant, and their annoyance was palpable. They discussed lecturers who did respond to spontaneous emails over the weekend. These lecturers were considered to be 'good teachers'. These were on-campus students for whom the lecturer, a close colleague of mine, had been readily available the previous week during class and contact time to answer any questions.*
>
> *I considered the following questions: These 'good teachers' may have been more immediately available, but were they better teachers? If students are asking questions at the very last minute about assessment, how had they been prepared for the task? Had the students been prepared adequately? Had the instructions been clear enough?*
>
> *I could foresee the negative comments on the student evaluations. This type of 'last-minute' contact had been happening to me a little, and I wondered how I might influence student expectations and action.*

This illustrates one of the issues with the 'unlevel playing field'. If everyone can set their own hours and respond when they want to students, students will evaluate academic practice using uneven criteria. This example illustrates the initial link between working hours, availability, evaluations, and perceived teaching quality.

The reality is that we can't, and probably shouldn't, be able to overly influence whether a peer is responding to students on weekends or late at night. We can, however, set expectations for students about when and how we will respond to them.

If my experience is anything to go by, restricting availability to students has improved student experience. It has come, however, with deep reflection on how to improve many other areas of my teaching. I have found that searching for efficiency has resulted in increased effectiveness.

Identifying our available hours and creating an 'ideal schedule' is the first step in taking some control of our life on the treadmill.

Chapter 3 summary and activities

In this chapter, we've explored academic time and the concept of building a fixed schedule within an environment that often has few boundaries. You should have calculated your hours, and created a schedule using those categories that would ideally work for you.

From here, we're going to investigate time thieves that provide the biggest challenge for academics. Time thieves are those things that make you run faster on the treadmill or make the tornado spin more wildly, with limited outcome. They are those things that affect efficiency and effectiveness.

Chapter 3 activity 1 - *calculate your hours*

The first step is to calculate your weekly hours. Quite simply:

> How many hours per week *should* you work (calculate so you have an average weekly rate)?

Once you have done this, calculate the following as a percentage of your weekly hours, based on your contract or conditions of work:

How many hours in that week *should* be research (if any)?
How many hours in that week *should* be teaching (if any)?
How many hours in that week *should* be service or engagement (if any)?

Note these hours somewhere prominent. You may come back to these quite frequently as you work your way through the chapters.

This activity is going to be tough for some of you. If you are not working full-time, but as a sessional casual, it is highly likely that you are doing a lot of work for free. You can do this exercise from a *'what would be ideal'* perspective, or from a *'what am I currently doing for free'* perspective. Either approach will potentially be illuminating.

Chapter 3 activity 2 - build your ideal schedule

Build a schedule that allocates time within a week to research/teaching/research that reflect the hours you *should* be allocating to those areas.

The only rule here is that you must make time for everything within the week. There's no *'I'll do all my research in the summer break'*. You need to allocate time into your weekly schedule.

Some of you will argue that it's impossible. For example, you may have a class time-table that requires you to teach in class for 16 hours, and your overall allocation for teaching is 16.5, leaving you no time for student consultation. We'll get to that later. At this point, build the picture of where you want to be - the schedule that would work for you if it worked, and was consistent with your conditions of employment and general workplace requirement (such as needing to be on campus a few days per week).

References and further reading

Gardiner, M. (n.d.). *Thinkwell Coaching*. Retrieved from https://www.ithinkwell.com.au
Newport, C. (2016). *Deep work: Rules for focused success in a distracted world*. London: Hachette.
Sang, K., Powell, A., Finkel, R., & Richards, J. (2015). 'Being an academic is not a 9-5 job': Long working hours and the 'ideal worker' in UK academia. *Labour & Industry: A Journal of the Social and Economic Relations of Work, 25*(3), 235-249. doi:10.1080/10301763.2015.1081723

Perspectives on work

Work-life balance is a contested notion. Read more about 'volunteerism and conscription' and perspectives on work hours:

Drago, R., Wooden, M., & Black, D. (2009). Long work hours: Volunteers and conscripts. *British Journal of Industrial Relations, 47*(3), 571-600. doi:10.1111/j.1467-8543.2009.00717.x
Thompson, J. A., & Bunderson, J. S. (2001). Work-nonwork conflict and the phenomenology of time: Beyond the balance metaphor. *Work and Occupations, 28*(1), 17-39. doi:10.1177/073088
8401028001003

34 *Academic time*

Balancing work-life in academia

American academic Tanya Golash-Boza maintains a blog piece on her blog getalifephd.blogspot.com titled 'What's the matter with a forty-hour work week for academics?' (2012). In it, she challenged the view that academics should be working 50-70-hour weeks, and outlined her personal schedule which included commitments with children. Her technique involved using the Pomodoro technique for focus (which I use when writing), and blocking work into chunks of time. I have followed Tanya's work for years because of her advocacy through her blog for having a life beyond the PhD and academic work. I was interested in the responses this particular post generated, particularly from readers from the UK who suggested that they had less control over what they could do with their classes, and from teaching academics who suggested that she lived in a bubble and her life didn't reflect the reality for teaching academics. Tanya acknowledged that she was working to a 40% teaching workload in a research institution. Her track record is impressive enough – as she notes herself, it contains books, publications, and edited collections in her discipline. She's a tenured professor at an 'R1' institution, which is the highest possible ranking for universities engaged in research in the United States. Read more at:

Golash-Boza, T. (2012). *What's the matter with a forty-hour work week for academics?* Retrieved from http://getalifephd.blogspot.com/2012/03/whats-matter-with-forty-hour-work-week.html.

Gudbjörg Rafnsdóttir and Thamar Heijstra write on the impact of workplace flexibility on work-family balance in academic life, particularly on women. They argue that flexibility can reproduce traditional power relations and gender-segregated division. Read more at:

Rafnsdóttir, G. L., & Heijstra, T. M. (2013). Balancing work – family life in academia: The power of time. *Gender, Work & Organization, 20*(3), 283-296. doi: 10.1111/j.1468-0432.2011.00571.x

Time as a budget

Alex Cavoulakos writes on productivity in work environments. She is not an academic, but has written on time as a budget. For example, 'How to Reclaim More Than 1,300 Minutes Each Week' (www.themuse.com/advice/how-to-reclaim-more-than-1300-minutes-each-week) includes links to downloadable spreadsheets that will help you calculate your hours generally.

4 What's your time thief?

Time thieves are those things that affect your ability to be efficient. From a 'treadmill and tornadoes' perspective, they result in unnecessary spin and create busy work.

It is impossible to list every time thief in academic life. Our daily routines are as diverse as there are people reading this book. This chapter focuses on time thieves that affect our efficiency associated with personal organisation, teaching organisation, and curriculum design. It represents learning from my experience as a teaching-focused academic trying to balance a busy life and produce research outcomes, and as a mentor of others trying to do the same.

Personal organisation

Some of us are naturally organised, while others must work hard to develop systems for creating a sense of order (I include myself in this category). Personal organisation is something we can control, and I won't spend too much time on this because it's well covered by other general time management books, some of which are mentioned at the end of this chapter.

The sheer volume of work that academics are required to manage, however, means that personal organisation is a variable in our ability to manage our workload. Examples of tornado-spinning activities related to personal organisation in academic contexts include:

- spending 30 minutes looking for an email you think was sent around three weeks ago about a topic that has re-emerged;
- looking for the contact details of someone you met at a conference but never took the time to store their details;
- looking for a file that you were sure you saved in one folder, but you're not sure of the date;
- finding that reference for a great article because you didn't take notes and its reference details at the time you were reading it;
- making changes to an earlier version of a document because you didn't appropriately manage version control;

36 *What's your time thief?*

- spending time looking for a room or building on campus because you didn't take the time to review a campus map *before* you set off to find it.

Ideas about how to prioritise what's most important versus urgent, and manage tools such as email and your calendar, are no different generally in academia with a few exceptions that I'll cover here. I am going to use examples to illustrate the interconnectedness of time-thieving in academic contexts in this chapter. I will focus most specifically on things that will have the most impact on increasing efficiency and effectiveness in the longer term.

Email

Brian is a Goth Studies PhD student who is teaching four classes across different universities. He is teaching an on-campus class for Jane, a full-time academic. Brian's contract includes some time for student contact and class preparation. He therefore provides his email address to students. Brian has told students he checks emails at the end of each day.

Jane is someone who responds to emails at all hours of the day. Students have learned that if they email Brian, they don't get an instant response during the day or late in the evening. They therefore email Jane, who responds on Brian's behalf and cc's him on the emails.

When Brian checks his email at night, he not only has emails from students, but responses from Jane. In many cases, Jane sends him an explanatory email to support the email she has sent directly to the student. Brian has to carefully read all emails. He decides not to respond to students because Jane has already done this. At the end of term, Jane is unhappy because student comments in the course feedback indicate that Brian was unresponsive to students.

Brian is on and affected by Jane's treadmill. His time, which could be better spent preparing for class, is spent on email. Worse still, as a casual academic, he is not getting paid for his work, and it's eating into his study time.

The issues at play here are:

- **Control and accountability.** Jane is feeling under pressure because student feedback affects her performance rating, so she is over-responsive to students.
- **Lack of email policy.** Students have quickly learned to exploit inconsistent approaches between Jane and Brian.
- **Conscription.** Brian feels that he is required to be available to students outside class, much of which is time for which he is not paid.

This example highlights the ways in which our work is interrelated with our peers. It also highlights the way in which email becomes a door into our personal room through which students can access our time and information about our courses/their study.

What's the spin factor?

There is no email strategy here. Email begets email, and more emails. Brian is caught in Jane's tornado. Students might feel responded to, but this is at Brian's and Jane's personal expense. Students have not been informed about appropriate use of email.

What's the treadmill speed?

Brian and Jane are sprinting with no end in sight while teaching is in session.

Email is a routine method of communication and is not going to go away anytime soon. In academic environments, we tend to leave our 'email door' open to students. This means we don't clearly establish and communicate boundaries as to our online availability. We fear that students will respond negatively and equate lack of responsiveness to poor teaching.

Another source of emails that 'build up' in academic environments are thought-based messages that aim to generate discussion. They might be thought bubbles that don't require response, but are records of thinking by members of a team on a particular issue.

Email is effective if used strategically to manage information. The following questions can determine appropriate uses:

- Do we need to create a record of conversation?
- Are we generating a new idea or thought we would like people to think about before a broader conversation?
- Do we need to include parties external to the organisation in an exchange that requires a decision?

In every case, the question should be 'How do we reduce email?' as opposed to 'How do we manage email?'. Anything that needs to be repeated to others on the same matter, and anything that's going to generate 'email tennis' resulting in repeat engagement on a minor routine matter, should be considered time theft.

Some people advocate for ignoring email. However, if you're smart with email use, you won't need to because you'll have a strategy to reduce email traffic. We'll talk about this in later chapters.

Chapter 4 - email activity

Reflect on how you use email. Answer the following specific questions, in detail.

1   Do you have scholarly conversations via email? How do you file them? Are they easy to retrieve? Do you record them in such a way that you could write a paper or blog post?

38   *What's your time thief?*

2   Think about your relationship between email and students. Do you respond to student email immediately, or do you ignore them?
3   Do you find yourself writing the same information repeatedly?

Spend a few minutes reflecting on *how* you use email now and how you might like to improve your use of email in the future. We'll come back to this.

Social media

Jonathon is a political science academic. He believes that he needs to be active on Twitter because he wants to know what is happening in political circles 'as it happens'. He loves being online, getting a sense of a story, and watching it unfold. He engages with students via Twitter and asks them to follow him so he can communicate with them all day. He receives good student satisfaction scores, but some complaints related to late return of essays.

This engagement is not assessed, and students are not asked to reflect on any aspect of their online discussion. When Jonathon is asked to complete an audit of his time, he finds that he spends almost 3 hours per day online. As a teaching-focused academic, he isn't under pressure to publish, but he finds it difficult to focus and hasn't written a research-based paper in 12 months. He suspects students who engage with him online perform better overall in their assignments. He doesn't know whether this is because they are more motivated generally, or because the online discussion promotes critical thinking.

The issues at play here are:

*   **Time wasting.** While it is reasonable to expect a political science academic to engage with political debate in the public sphere, the amount of time spent is excessive.
*   **Wasted assessment opportunity.** Student engagement with political issues online is valuable, but is not assessed.
*   **Wasted scholarship opportunity.** There's a research question here about student engagement that could be subject of a journal article or inform teaching practice.

Social media has a reputation as a time thief, and there is no doubt it is if not used correctly – as I would argue is the case with Jonathon.

What's the spin factor?

Jonathon is spinning daily, but with a bit of deliberate action, could invert this tornado so that the spin is reduced and outputs are increased.

What's the treadmill speed?

Jonathon is setting his own pace here. He's not necessarily suffering, but he isn't winning any academic race.

The potential for us to lose hours of our day into the vortex of social media is well-recognised. In August 2016, two articles were published in *The Times Higher Education*, an online publication, that highlighted the two opposing camps. Andy Miah published his article first, titled 'Why academics should make time for social media'. A week later, Gabriel Egan presented the counter-view, writing 'Why academics should *not* make time for social media'.

Neither of these pieces are particularly scholarly, and neither are based on anything substantial such as empirical evidence, but they do represent the polarised views on the issue. Cal Newport also talks about social media in his book *Deep Work*. He recommends giving up social media with a caveat that some people may need to use it for specific reasons.

Surprisingly little research, however, has been done on the impact of using social media on areas of work that influence an academic career. It is hard research to do. How do you measure the relationship between sharing links to articles on Twitter and download or citation? A few have tried, and there is evidence that engaging with Twitter can positively affect the profile of your work. Some examples are provided in the section on further readings.

Many academics avoid engagement in/with/on social media because they don't know how to use it correctly, or consider it one more thing to do. Others, like Jonathon, spend all day on it and would acknowledge that they have fallen into the trap of 'addiction'. If you follow me on Twitter or LinkedIn, you can certainly see I engage during the day, but it's only while I'm in commute, waiting for a meeting to start (when no-one else is in the room), or while I am waiting for something to download courtesy of Australia's notoriously slow internet speed.

Social media is a time thief if it traps you in non-essential social conversations, and draws you into a vortex of connection from which you find it difficult to extract yourself. If you are using it for teaching, it can also be a time thief if you find yourself engaging with your students all day every day on Facebook. In Jonathon's case, it is useful because it means he is up to date with current events, but he could probably be current at an hour of use per day rather than three. A much better use of his time would be to spend 2 hours reflecting on the political activities of the day making notes, with a view to publish commentary or capture data from which research could be published.

The question to ask about social media use is: '*How can I make it more productive with less (or limited) effort?*', rather than '*How can I manage my social media use?*'.

Chapter 4 - social media activity

Reflect on your personal social media use.

1   Track your social media use in a day. Including personal and work-based use (teaching/ dissemination of information), how many minutes/hours do you spend using social media?
2   Do you think you use social media strategically, or do you just use it for the sake of keeping up to date? If neither of these reasons apply, why do you use it?

40   *What's your time thief?*

3   Identify one or two 'moments' that made your social media use worthwhile.
4   Do you have a method for tracking data on a particular issue of interest? Would this be a good idea and assist you with scholarship?

Travel

> Suraya is a contracted associate lecturer in business. She has recently completed an industry-focused teaching scholarship. In the previous year, she presented at four conferences on her innovations in teaching practice, and this year, she's on track for the same amount. Last year, she did not convert any of her presentations into journal articles, and it is looking to be the same again this year. Suraya's mentor has advised her that she needs to contain her conference attendance and travel, and focus on writing journal articles. Suraya feels conflicted. She has met a lot of people and is getting a lot of ideas for future research.

The issues at play here are:

- **Lack of 'impact' strategy.** Conferences can feel great, but unless you're an invited keynote, don't necessarily have a lot of impact when it comes to promotion or tenure.
- **Administrative burden.** Every trip creates an administrative load – requests, approvals, fund acquittal, reservations, confirmations, and so on.
- **Idea overload.** It's great to get ideas, but too many are a distraction. It's easy, in conversation, to be sidelined or attracted by other agendas.

What's the spin factor?

Suraya is not being strategic about her conference attendance. She is spending a lot of time burdened by travel administration, losing time in travel, and presenting at conferences for which she doesn't get recognised when it comes to promotion or tenure. She's getting a lot of new ideas, which are distracting her. She could invert this tornado by linking conference attendance with writing papers.

What's the treadmill speed?

Suraya is sprinting. She could slow her speed but have greater impact by focusing on writing journal articles, and strategically selecting conferences at which she can present completed results.

Suraya is not alone in her dilemma. Networking, sharing our research, and getting ideas is an exciting and necessary part of our work. Travel, however, and everything that goes with it, can be a time thief if the overall impact on our workload and the overall value of that travel is not considered.

What's your time thief? 41

In Suraya's case, the questions to ask are:

- Do we need to go to four conferences? Would two be enough?
- Is the reason we are going related to 'fear of missing out'? If so, is there another way of creating/fostering contacts?
- Is conference attendance and the administrative burden that goes with it worth it?
- What would be the impact of converting the time you would have spent travelling on research and writing a journal paper?

Conference presentations can be strategic. They create clear deadlines for full papers to be written, help us focus our thoughts on aspects of our work, and allow us to make important personal connections. There's a strong argument, however, that junior academics should target no more than two conferences per year and concentrate on research and journal article writing. In Suraya's case, conference papers aren't going to make her competitive when a permanent job becomes available, but journal articles will. Unless she is very good at converting her conference papers to journal articles, or has perfected the practice of writing a full paper and submitting it to a journal prior to presenting at a conference, travel is a time thief.

The 'big' conferences set their dates and themes well in advance. You should be able to plan well ahead for conference travel, and then focus your attention on writing papers for journals.

Chapter 4 - travel activity

1   How much travel do you do per year for academic work? Reflect on your previous year - what were the outcomes of any travel? List any new contacts (and outcomes associated with that), or conference papers that were published in *refereed* proceedings or were 'pre-runs' of journal articles subsequently published.
2   How much time did you spend on this travel, in hours? Could that time have been better spent on other important tasks?
3   Look at the year ahead. Can you define two important conferences that could be your focus? If you make the decision to say 'no' to others that come your way unless it fits directly into your work, how else might you fulfil your networking requirements?

Reflect in your journal. You may decide at the end of this that travel IS important to you and you do want to attend all these conferences. If so, calculate the real time associated with this and include it into your workload.

When it comes to personal organisation, questions related to email, social media, and travel are the three most prominent I encounter when talking to peers; thus, the attention given to them here. The next section will cover time thieves associated with teaching administration.

42   *What's your time thief?*

Overcommitment

As a new PhD graduate, Carol is a newly appointed faculty aiming for a tenured position. She is a 'newbie', but is also a 'prepper'. Her workload allocation is consistent with a normal full-time balanced academic. She is reluctant to say no to any requests in the hope that she will build her overall portfolio.

In the past month, Carol has committed to running a first-year student experience session teaching poetry as a 'campus enhancement experience' (3 hours per week, including prep, setup, and walking across campus), agreed to be a pastoral care adviser for first-year creative writing students (2 hours per week), reviewed one journal article (2 hours), and created an online creative writing publication to promote student work, working with senior students every week to assist edit and curate work (5 hours per week). This online publication is not linked to assessment, but Carol thinks there is potential that it could be.

Carol has received another request to review a journal article, and an invitation to speak at a local community writing group about study in creative writing. She has also been asked to contribute to a review of the Humanities curriculum. This includes writing a benchmarking report that will require some research into what is being offered in other programmes.

It is currently Week 5 of term. She feels she is already at breaking point.

The issues at play here are:

- **Overload.** These activities, when combined with Carol's required hours of teaching, put her at significant overload. It is physically impossible for Carol to complete everything *within* her fixed schedule. She doesn't realise this, because she has not completed a review of hours. If she had, she would realise that she only has 8 hours per week to devote to 'service', and she has committed herself to 10 hours' service as a minimum.
- **Strategy.** Carol is saying yes to everything without prioritising those things that will ultimately benefit her the most when it comes to tenure.

Overcommitment happens when we aren't conscious of how long things will take us to do, we underestimate the size of a task, or the task isn't particularly transparent. Service is the focus of this example. It is an important component of academic life but is rarely defined.

What's the spin factor?

Carol is spinning uncontrollably here. Carol's 10-plus hours of service mean she will be marking and doing her teaching work at night or on weekends. She is not making the most of opportunities available to combine service and teaching.

What's the treadmill speed?

Carol is at risk of falling off the back of the treadmill. As it is mid-term, she can't slow it, but needs to find a way to take short breaks to catch her breath.

What's your time thief? 43

Examining what your treadmill looks like on a weekly or monthly basis will assist with overcommitment. We can't take on another task if we can't fit it in.

As an example, I have already mentioned that at time of writing I am involved with supervision of six RhD students, four of whom I supervise as principal supervisor. I will only take on new students as my current students complete, as I am at capacity.

I know this because I schedule regular meetings with the PhD students for whom I am principal supervisor every fortnight on Monday afternoons – between 1 p.m. and 5 p.m. I review any set work on Monday mornings. I can clearly see, therefore, that I can't schedule any more students in, and because we meet regularly, the pieces I review aren't huge documents that require me to routinely take myself offline for hours.

When we're coming to a big milestone, such as confirmation or submission, I will schedule more blocks of time to review work. Masters and doctoral study is supposed to be independent research, supported by a supervisor. Setting students small, achievable tasks that guide them forward while still promoting independence has been a successful strategy for me.

It's an example of controlling the treadmill – each fortnight, we take a moment collectively to stop, discuss, review, and move forward. It appears time consuming, but saves significant time in the longer term because it prevents students from getting lost along the way, ensures everyone is familiar with issues and moving forward, and saves time in trying to schedule those 'are you available?' meetings.

I know that a journal paper review will take me roughly half a day. I now only review a maximum of one per month, because I must also read other papers daily in my managerial role. Knowing that this time is restricted prompts me to push back if I already have one journal review under way and I am requested to return the review within a few weeks. These are the one thing for which I am sometimes late, because journal reviews are at the bottom of my list in terms of workload priority, and I don't work on these in my personal time.

Chapter 4 – overcommitment activity

List all the things with which you are currently involved from a work perspective. Don't just identify what you're doing. Think about why you're doing it. Be honest. See the following commitment table as an example.

Commitment table

Activity	Category	Hours	Why?
Teaching – class sessions	Teaching	20 hours per week	Core duties
School meetings	Service (internal)	2 hours per month	Visibility/peer engagement
Journal review	Service (external)	3 hours per month	Esteem factor – seen as important for promotion as evidence of your standing in discipline
Student support hours for first-year students	Service (internal)	2 hours per week	Because no-one else will, but it's important to help students succeed early in their study career
Mentoring peers	Service (internal)	1 hour per week	Not recognised, but I think it's important

44   *What's your time thief?*

This becomes your 'onto the treadmill edges for a breath' moment. You may find that you are doing multiple tasks for the same reason. Or, as previously mentioned, you may find that you're doing something because no-one else will. Once you have completed your list, discuss it with a mentor.

Start thinking about what you really want or need to keep, and if you are going to keep things, how you are going to make this work more strategically for you from a time/impact perspective.

Teaching organisation

Teaching administration

Kevin is a biology professor who runs a large first-year course. He has had a sudden heart attack mid-term. He has survived, but required heart surgery. He will not return for some time and is too unwell to communicate with peers. There are 900 students in his class, including those whom he instructs directly, and 20 lab tutors. It is two weeks before a compulsory residential school that Kevin was responsible for organising. Kevin's course assistant, who is casual, is currently on a week's leave prior to the intensive teaching session.

Kevin's Head of School has requested assistance from Huiling, a more junior biology academic who convenes her own course. She is happy to help as Kevin was her PhD supervisor and one of her mentors. When she steps in to help, however, she is unable to access any course materials as they are on Kevin's laptop computer. No centrally located backup can be found including information regarding the residential school sessions.

Huiling requested access to Kevin's online course so she can see what materials are available, but has found that he uploads material after sessions to encourage students to come to class. There is no information related to upcoming classes. She has no record of who the tutors are and is waiting for the school administration to identify all tutors contracted to teach into Kevin's course.

Students are complaining that their work has not been marked (they need this to be done prior to them coming to the residential school). Huiling estimates it will be a few days before she has everything 'under control'. In the meantime, she is required to continue teaching her own courses.

The issues at play here are:

- **Problem transferral.** Kevin's problem is unavoidable, but the way in which it manifests quickly to become anothers' problem is not. That it specifically transfers to a more junior academic with their own workload to manage is, I would suggest, common in some work environments.
- **Lack of information management workplace policy.** That everything is on Kevin's personal laptop with no backup, and that Huiling must wait for information to be

'found', indicates a problem with knowledge management associated with teaching in this faculty.

- **Lack of backup for a large class.** While Kevin has one assistant, the casualised workforce that supports this class results in a loss of knowledge for the organisation at times like this.

What's the spin factor?

Kevin isn't spinning. It has all become too much for him. Huiling has been drawn into the organisational tornado here. It is likely that she will lose her own momentum for many weeks.

What's the treadmill speed?

Huiling was travelling nicely. She is organised and professional. She has suddenly had to jump onto someone else's treadmill at maximum speed.

This case provides an example of how a workload can suddenly explode. In this case, its explosion is fuelled by lack of personal organisation by Kevin, or perhaps a requirement by the school to keep critical records in a central location (such as tutor lists, timetables, core teaching materials).

It's also an example of workload that's not accounted for. It is 'service' and may amount, for Huiling, for up to 40 hours (and beyond), but I'll bet it won't be counted on any promotion or tenure application. The cynic in me suggests that at best, Huiling may be recognised for being collegial.

This example is extreme, but illustrates the point. More routine examples of problem transferral, when someone else's problem becomes ours in such a way that our time is affected, include:

- A student is late to class because they slept in (their problem) and wants us to stay behind and explain what they missed (affects our time).
- A peer routinely doesn't respond to students or come to campus (their problem), so students are always emailing you or coming to see you to ask about that peer's courses (impacts on our time).

This may appear simplistic. In cases such as Kevin's, it is entirely legitimate that we step in to assist with someone else's problem. Our challenge is to identify those problems that are important for us to assist with, and ways to make our support more efficient when we do provide it.

Chapter 4 - teaching administration activity

1   Reflect on Kevin and Huiling's dilemma. If you were to suddenly get ill, how would your peers be able to support you? Is your course information stored in

46 *What's your time thief?*

a cloud-based centralised setting, or is it all on your laptop or on USB drives? If everything is 'everywhere', spend time to organise your files and teaching-related information so it could be easily handed over, grouping them into categories such as Admin, Teaching Modules, Student Information, and Extra Resources (or similar).

2   If you are really organised, is your information in a central repository? If not, take the time to find out how this could happen within your department by making a note to discuss this with your supervisor.

Student communication

Arun is a very organised chemistry academic. He reads a lot and has lots of light-bulb moments for his students. He uses a learning management system (Moodle) to support his teaching, which includes online and on-campus students. He uploads links to this site as term progresses via a 'Useful Links' section.

By the end of term, there are 93 links associated with news articles in the 'Useful Links' section. Arun makes reference to one of them in a lecture. This lecture is recorded for online students. Only 15 people out of 60 attended the lecture. In the weeks following the session, Arun receives 23 emails from students enrolled in his class advising him that they are unable to find the link. Arun checks - it is there, but buried among others. He responds individually to every student who emailed, advising them of the same point and giving them all the direct link. He is also receiving emails from students asking him whether these readings are compulsory (they are not). The readings are not assessed.

Arun also likes to schedule online sessions when he can for online students. He sets them a few weeks in advance, but the dates and times change depending on his availability. The sessions are not regular and simply for discussion so online students can ask him questions.

Arun's student evaluations at the end of term reflect that students found information hard to find, which surprises him because he has deliberately created a section of useful links. His students didn't appreciate his willingness to support them, despite the fact that he scheduled extra online sessions to support students.

The issues at play here are:

- **Information overload.** There is potentially too much information being generated by Arun. Students are feeling overwhelmed and are in turn overwhelming him.
- **Lack of curation.** The value of simply uploading/promoting links on an ad hoc basis is questionable. There are better ways to do things.
- **Lack of consolidated communication channel and policy.** Arun is making individual contact with students, saying the same thing repeatedly. He has not established a way to communicate with all students (on-campus and online) to disseminate information in an orderly and considered fashion.

What's your time thief? 47

- **Lack of structure in communication.** Arun thinks he is being responsive and available to students by scheduling ad hoc open sessions. This is creating pressure for him, however, and stress for students who can't predict in advance when a session will be held.

What's the spin factor?

Anything that generates unnecessary work is spin. The touchdown effect of the intellectual work Arun is doing is limited, so there's a lot of topspin for minimal positive outcome, for him and his students. With consideration this tornado could easily be inverted.

What's the treadmill speed?

Arun is generating his own speed, and it's much faster than it needs to be.

This example relates to teaching materials (links), but also communication practice. Communicating with our students accounts for an enormous amount of our time. It is particularly problematic if we are communicating with them in multiple places – in lectures, then online, via discussion forums, via emails, in hallways, and via social media. This is complicated by the fact that increasingly, our students don't come to class. They try to engage with the online versions of our courses, but in some cases, half-heartedly. Once they realise that this takes more effort, they will try to short-cut and ask staff and peers for assistance.

It is important to create a sense of order for students. This requires us to think about what is important for them. The question to ask here is not: *'How do I manage student communication?'*. Rather, we should ask two questions:

1   *'How do I streamline communication so that I only need to say something once for students?'*
2   *'What do students really need to know to pass their assessment and extend themselves if they want to?'*

Chapter 4 – communication activity

Reflect on the way in which you communicate with students. Do you support your teaching with a learning management system? Do you have a system for communication with online and on-campus students? How do you ensure that all students receive the same information? Is there room for improvement?

Bushfire management

In addition to running her on-campus classes, Jane has established a discussion forum that students can access to discuss course content or assessment.

48   *What's your time thief?*

Within the first few weeks of term, she notices that one student is consistently asking questions that she is covering in class. Jane responds immediately to these questions, but they always trigger a follow-up question. The student is challenging the premise of some of the content – she suggests that the readings are old and that some of the content is irrelevant. Jane has carefully curated the course's materials. The older readings are seminal; that is, they were selected because they represented points of view at a time, or were considered part of a discipline's 'canon'. The student is very rude in her tone. No ground rules were established with regard to acceptable behaviour on the discussion forum at the beginning of term.

Jane checks with the on-campus tutor who is taking the class for whom the student has registered, only to find that the student has not attended any class to this point. Because the student hasn't been attending class, she has not been present during discussion about the readings, so is reviewing them online without context.

Some students are responding on Jane's behalf, advising that the readings have been discussed in class. Other students, however, are agreeing with this student, and are starting to also complain about other aspects of the class.

Jane is having to spend increasing time 'defending' her approach and responding to online discussion. She is spending time talking to tutors who are now being challenged by students in class. Some are getting upset because they are not paid for the time they are spending out of class dealing with student issues.

Jane's allocated time for teaching has now expanded by an extra 2–3 hours per week dealing with this issue.

The issues at play here are:

- **Lack of ground rules for engagement.** The student feels confident to challenge the teacher in a public forum in a manner that could be considered rude.
- **Engagement tennis.** Because the student has initiated engagement via the discussion forum, Jane has responded via the same means. This results in 'to-and-fro' communication that is not as efficient as it could be.

What's the spin factor?

Jane is spinning unnecessarily, with minimal effect, because of concerns of a small but vocal number of students.

What's the treadmill speed?

Jane's speed is being influenced by students. If she took stock, and stepped off the treadmill, she may be able to halt the complaint cancer spreading within the student cohort.

Dealing with complaints eats into planned activities because they are usually unexpected. They can be made at any time, and depending on who they are made to, will require us to stop what we are doing and respond to that complaint.

What's your time thief? 49

Complaints can be from students, staff, or industry partners. Student complaints are wide ranging. They might be prompted by a concern that a lecturer didn't respond to a student email, didn't provide enough guidance on an exam or essay question, didn't provide enough feedback or explain a grade – the list can be quite extensive. Students will often complain to more than one person, meaning multiple people will be included in emails, and need to be back-briefed on any responses.

Some complaints are extremely serious; for example, allegations of sexual assault, harassment, and misconduct. While they are time-consuming, I don't consider these time thieves as a general comment. They are genuine and some may be referred to the police. However, they are related to behaviour, which is in turn related to culture.

This leads me to the most critical point. The time thief may be the complaint, but behaviour, such as being rude, dismissive, arrogant, unkind, or inappropriate, triggers the complaint. Not responding to emails for days or weeks on end with no acknowledgement is behaviour-related. So is being regularly late to class, not returning assignments on time without explanation, and so on. Students have a right to complain about genuine issues.

Chapter 4 – bushfire management activity

Reflect on a 'bushfire' event if it has happened to you. Some of the questions to consider are:

- What happened?
- Why did it happen?
- What could you have done to prevent it?
- What extra work did it generate, and how much extra time and effort resulted for you?
- What can you do to pre-empt problems and/or prevent it happening again?
- Are you able to create a checklist that would help you prepare/prevent such a bushfire?
- What responsibility did you have for the bushfire, and if you lack overall control, what actions can you take in your position to reduce the impact?

We will return to this topic in Chapter 5.

Curriculum design
Teaching materials

Jonathon has set a new textbook for his political science course which comes with instructor resources, slides, and test questions. It is published by a major publisher, but it is a UK text. Jonathon plans to set some locally based case studies to complement the text's theoretical focus, but his workshop activities are largely based on those set within the text. In-class tests are drawn from the text's online test bank. Jonathon's assignment questions are based on the text's content, whereby he asks

50 *What's your time thief?*

students to apply the theory to current issues. He uses the textbook PowerPoint slides in his lectures.

This is easy for Jonathon. The textbook covers a lot of required content, so he doesn't need to think too much about what he needs to 'teach'. This leaves him available to communicate with students on social media, engaging with them about local matters.

Everything is going well during term, but students are starting to complain that the context is British and has limited relevance to the local context. Jonathon has found limited time to create the local case studies he was intending. Additionally, when reviewing essays for assessment 1, he finds a high incidence of copying when he checks the students' Turnitin scores (Turnitin is a well-known copy-detection platform that integrates with many learning management systems). Out of 125 students, he finds that 15 have copied directly from other assignments. He is not sure if the students have copied from one another within the course in his classes, or have purchased an assignment from an 'essay mill'. Jonathon must investigate each incidence. Each will take him a minimum of 2 hours, and must be completed within two weeks to satisfy university policy. Suddenly, Jonathon has an extra 30 hours' work.

Students are starting to complain about everything publicly to Jonathon, in conversation on social media.

The issues at play here are:

- **Lazy curriculum design.** Jonathon's over-reliance on a textbook as the basis of his teaching might appear to reduce a teaching load, but comes with its own inherent set of problems.
- **Teaching-centred rather than student-centred approach.** Relying on content delivered by textbook as a teaching approach misses an opportunity for authentic learning.
- **Contextualisation is dismissed.** Students want to contextualise knowledge. The selection of a textbook that uses foreign examples is always problematic.
- **Assumption of available time.** Jonathon assumed that he would have time to develop some case studies during term. He didn't prioritise these, however, and did not complete these as a complement to the set textbook. This should have been anticipated and completed prior to the term commencing.

What's the spin factor?

The spin started quite spontaneously here and gained intensity quickly. The time taken to investigate student cheating and respond to complaints could have been anticipated, and will affect all other parts of Jonathon's life.

What's the treadmill speed?

Jonathon thought he was running quite slowly. He was feeling relaxed enough to be engaging with students via social media. It's clear, though, that taking a few pauses to consider curriculum design would have prevented the treadmill from suddenly reaching maximum pace.

As many of us know, once a complaint mindset sets in within a student cohort, it can be hard to recover. In this case, regardless of the merit of the text, Jonathon may potentially lose credibility – even if he is popular with those students with whom he communicates as 'friends' on social media.

What looked like an easy choice, which was developing a course around an existing textbook, has turned into a nightmare – and the time spent investigating allegations of cheating is unexpected, but necessary. The textbook Jonathon has set is also the text for many other similar courses, and contract cheaters or essay mills have samples of the set essay available for sale.

The question here to ask is: '*What is a more effective approach to selecting and using teaching materials?*'.

Chapter 4 – teaching materials activity

Reflect on your use of teaching materials.

1   Do you rely on a textbook to teach students?
2   Are any of your materials problematic?
3   Could you ask students to suggest/use/research/generate materials for use in a course?

Note that this is not suggesting that textbooks aren't useful. I certainly use a couple in my courses, but I am very deliberate about when and how I use them.

Lecture preparation

Huiling is filling in for Kevin, our biology professor, and has been able to access his teaching material. She has found his lectures, and notes that on many occasions, his lectures include reference to current discoveries in biology. In some cases, he has referenced his own work, but in others, he has drawn on published research findings. For example, Huiling has found a lecture on a development in 3D printing of human organs from 2017 and another from 2018. These are interesting but need another update. She knows it is good practice to include relevant information for students so they can make links between theory and current practice. She considers using the recorded lectures from last term, but these are 'dated' because the lecture is referring to 'this year', 'this week', and 'today' when discussing then-newly discovered information.

Updating lecture material is time-consuming as she searches for the latest information to include. She finds herself spending 3–4 hours preparing for her lectures each week to creating interesting materials. However, she considers that the class is large and the time is worth it. She delivers the lectures, which are recorded. Few

52   *What's your time thief?*

students turn up to class. There is no deliberate link between lectures and assessment - that is, students do not need to attend to pass. She doesn't do anything else with the material even though she has the intention to do so.

She wonders if there is a better way.

The issues at play here are:

- **Teacher-centric approach.** The liability is on Huiling to do all the work here. If we know that we learn best by teaching others, why aren't students doing the research and being assessed on this? Couldn't the students do the updating and be assessed on their discussion?
- **Hamster-wheel delivery.** Huiling knows that she should capture the knowledge in writing, or find a way to add value to her case studies. She always gets caught up with 'other stuff'. Taking extra care to write the cases up would enable Huiling to draw upon the knowledge in future terms, or better still, provide initial insights for students who can then conduct further research.
- **Repeated work with lack of foresight.** The research Huiling is doing amounts to research, scholarship, and currency. They could build up as an overview of history - for example, Huiling and Kevin could be tracking annual development of 3D biological printing. At this stage, however, it's a potential opportunity lost. We will discuss this specifically in later chapters.

What's the spin factor?

This is unnecessary spin that could be inverted by taking a more student-centric approach whereby Huiling could do less work and have greater impact. In this case, Huiling is spinning to create good lectures that students may or may not attend and watch. These lectures are interesting but aren't directly linked to assessment, so are considered by students as a 'nice to have', but not essential.

What's the treadmill speed?

The treadmill speed is constant here, but is self-generated. Forcing herself to step off, think ahead, and transfer some of the responsibility for learning would potentially slow the speed for everyone involved in the teaching of this course in the longer term.

Academic work involves developing, curating, and delivering knowledge which becomes 'content' for our classes. While many of us don't like to think about what we do as a commodity or product, we do create artefacts - lectures, study guides, tutorial exercises, workshop materials.

Dedicated teachers will spend a lot of time creating artefacts for our students, pulling together the best ideas on a topic interspersed with commentary and analysis. Some of

What's your time thief? 53

us are lucky enough to be experts in our field, and therefore have the luxury of being able to contribute to courses around knowledge we have been central in developing.

Developing learning materials is a necessary and valuable part of our work. As online delivery is becoming more popular, some of us find ourselves under increasing pressure to develop content for online courses, or as content that can be accessed by our on-campus students unable to attend class. Students are also becoming used to ubiquitous content - they know they can either come to class OR download the lecture/PowerPoint slides from a learning management system or content portal. The days of writing a lecture the week prior to delivering it (or even the day before) are therefore over for most of us. I know in my case, we are required to have the full 12 weeks' worth of materials ready for students at the beginning of a term because of our online delivery mode.

Quite simply, I see this part of my job as time theft if I repeat basic work every term. It's like being on the treadmill and never getting any fitter, suffering the same consequences every time. Our goal is to be incrementally more streamlined with our content every term until we have a course that is 'set and support'.

In Huiling's case, the research she does each week to update her course materials could be incorporated into building research cases, and could be 'time-neutral'. I'll deal with this as a tornado-inverting strategy in Chapter 6. The questions to ask when preparing lectures or class content are: *'How can I future-proof this so that I could use this next year or the year after?'*. This will change the way you plan, capture, curate, and deliver your material.

Chapter 4 activity - lecture preparation activity

Some questions for reflection here are:

1 How much time do you spend preparing lectures or workshops?
2 Do you simply pull out the slides or notes from last year, without adding value?
3 What steps do you take to make it easy for yourself to reuse or repurpose your material or research (if at all)?

Assessment design

Leah coordinates a course in introductory creative writing. Drafting is important to writing, and Leah has incorporated some drafts into her assessment design. One of the drafts is required early, meeting her faculty requirement that one assessment piece be due in the first four weeks.

Leah's assessment schedule for her creative writing course looks like this:

- *Tutorial exercises/online discussion - 10%*
- *Assignment 1 (Draft), due week 3 - 10%*
- *Assignment 1 (Creative Piece 1), due week 6 - 30%*

54 *What's your time thief?*

- *Assignment 2 (Draft), due week 9 - 10%*
- *Assignment 2 (Creative Piece 2), due week 12 - 40%*

There are 105 students in the class, and each draft takes a minimum of 20 minutes to review for Assignment 1, and 30 minutes for Assignment 2. The assessment requirements are the same between on-campus and online students. On-campus students complete writing exercises in class. Online students are required to submit their responses to the activities on a course discussion board. These writing activities aren't specifically related to the larger assignments.

From Week 3, Leah is marking. It is clear, however, that some students haven't read the unit profile, so some have missed the requirement to submit a compulsory draft. Leah spends the first half of Week 4 contacting students who haven't submitted their first assessment.

Upon submission of Assignment 1, students haven't taken as much notice of feedback as they could have.

This means that Leah is making the same comments as she did on the draft. Students are not required to address feedback (that is, what they did to improve their writing) as part of their submission. Students are asked to share their work in public, but many have resisted, saying they are too scared for others to read it.

Leah is frustrated.

By the time she is marking the Assignment 2 drafts, she's running late and has lost patience. In some cases, she provides no constructive feedback, and makes direct comments that are interpreted by students to be 'rude'. Students have started to complain on the student discussion board that they haven't received their assignments back in time to improve their final submissions. Others are complaining that when they did receive feedback, it was simply a grade with reference to a rubric - no specific feedback was included.

Even though students have had the opportunity to come to class and have their work privately reviewed, they have not done this - rather, they decided that they will submit exercise responses to the discussion board as online students, and have sought Leah's advice during her consultation hours as individuals. She has not seen some students at all, and has seen some students many times.

At the end of term, she receives six requests for reviews of grades on the basis of incorrect addition of marks. Feedback from one of the students suggested that the reason so many of the final assignments were poor was because students had worked out that they didn't have to 'do much to pass' if they had passed the drafts and tutorial exercises. They were able to concentrate on other assignments for other courses due at the same time. She also finds out that many students had taken the class as an elective because it was the only one that didn't have an exam.

By the end of term, Leah hates every minute of being at work. She's dispirited about the lack of passion exhibited by most students in class. She had been looking forward to being a full-time creative writing teacher.

What's your time thief? 55

The issues at play here are:

- **Too much individual assessment.** There are multiple pieces of assessment, all of which have a specific 'mark'. The number of tasks and marks allocated raise the risk of miscalculation at the end of term.
- **Arbitrary marks.** The marks allocated to assessment pieces don't reflect the time on task.
- **Sticking to principles and ignoring human factors.** Leah's assessment design is targeted at some human factors (students will focus on activities on which they are assessed), but ignores some others (students won't read the requirements of assessment, and will do what is easy, such as staying at home and posting responses to information online).
- **Limited scaffolding/relationship between assessment pieces.** There are many opportunities in this course to scaffold assessment. Students are not required to reflect on feedback and articulate what they did to make their writing better.

What's the spin factor?

Leah started spinning when she designed the assessment, and the size of the tornado grew exponentially from week 3, with effective touchdown only for those students who are genuinely interested in creative writing as a career or genuine interest. She is wasting a lot of time and effort catering to those who have a much more pragmatic view of study. The good news is that this tornado is quite easy to invert.

What's the treadmill speed?

This is a treadmill generated by assessment design because of the issues stated earlier. Leah is sprinting from an early start. She may not survive the session.

This is an interesting case because its essential design, which incorporates formative assessment in the form of drafts, reflects good practice. Leah's approach generally looks, on the surface, to be effective. It is working for the students who care, but there are many students who don't, and it's not working for her.

The questions to ask here are not about assignment management, which might be: *'How can I manage these assignments better?'*. Rather, the questions are: *'How can I encourage the students to read the assignment requirements?'* (assess their ability to attend to submission requirements); *'How can I reduce my marking requirement?'* (think creatively about what you're asking students to do); *'How can I increase the standard of submissions?'* (scaffold assessment); and *'What will be effective if I assume students aren't going to come to class and won't read the requirements?'* (find effective ways to embed critical requirements into assessment *efficiently*).

The hour we might spend marking one very poorly written piece because a student didn't come to class when we were explaining the requirements of the task is an hour we

56 *What's your time thief?*

don't get back. Their decisions should not affect our lives to our detriment. In my experience, some academics refuse to budge on principle - they expect students to come to class, and take notice of feedback. If we accept that they won't unless we assess it, we can change the ballgame. Chapter 7 explores ways to help improve our assessment design. We certainly don't want to be doing more assessment; we do want it to be more effective *and* efficient.

Chapter 4 activity - assessment design

1   Select a course that you are teaching. How many pieces of assessment are required? Are they scaffolded - that is, do they build on each other? Do you allocate marks to assessment manually, or is this automatic?
2   Focus, when you are reflecting on your assignments, on what takes the most time. Is it the time it takes to make comments on your assignments? If you don't make comments on your assignments, is it the time you take to address student complaints? Is it the reviews of grades? Is it the time it takes you to access the technology or learning management system? List these as individual items to identify those things that occupy the most of your time.

The next chapter will focus on how we might address some of the issues associated with assessment design, such as marking.

Technology

Kevin has returned from his sick leave and is preparing for another term.

Huiling, who has been filling in for him, has suggested he incorporate some virtual reality and augmented reality technology into his class. This, she posits, will increase student interest in what they are learning, and there is evidence that these technologies are particularly effective in science courses.

Students who are studying online would also benefit from this, because there is potential to incorporate this technology into assessment and increase the authenticity of learning. Kevin has never used augmented or virtual reality, and thinks it's just a gimmick, a fad that will pass. He rejects the idea.

Huiling decides to adopt some virtual reality into her classes. She uses some professional development money to learn about how to develop resources. She starts slowly, working with the university's learning and teaching department to development modules and illustrative examples. Huiling's teaching results are better - her students are not only more satisfied; their results have improved.

Kevin finds he is under pressure because students are comparing his learning resources with his peers. As an older academic, Kevin continues to resist the need for professional development in anything technology-related. He still has difficulty formatting Microsoft Word documents, and insists on printing off

What's your time thief? 57

all assignments, marking by hand, scanning them, and uploading them into the learning management system.

He knows he could be more efficient, but he is happy with his approach. The time he spends investing in the latest teaching tools is better spent on his lab research anyway. Kevin is resentful of the pressure being applied by Huiling. As a professor, he is senior to her, and it is likely that he will be on a promotion or tenure committee with influence on Huiling's career at some point.

The Dean has allocated some funds to develop innovative teaching materials. Because Kevin's class is one of the biggest, with a significant failure rate, he wants Kevin to engage with some of the new technologies.

The issues at play here are:

- **Peer pressure.** Students will compare approaches between different teachers. Kevin, as a professor, has decided that he would prefer to spend his time conducting research.
- **Resistance to learning.** Despite evidence that incorporating technology into the classroom is effective, Kevin is displaying resistance to learning new technologies that could improve student experience in his classroom.
- **Control.** Kevin feels that he has lost control. He is being forced to engage with new ways of teaching despite his resistance.

What's the spin factor?

Kevin is being forced to spin against his wishes.

What's the treadmill speed?

Kevin's treadmill is currently still, but he is aware that there is the potential for it to speed up exponentially – with someone else controlling the speed.

Technology is a double-edged sword in academic life. On the one hand, it provides us with tools that enable us. On the other hand, it takes time to learn, particularly if we need to get to a stage of mastery.

The very simple problem for academics is that workload allocation assumes that technology makes life easier and we should therefore be more efficient as a result. Quite the opposite is true. We know, for example, that teaching distance education requires more effort than teaching students traditionally in a face-to-face class (Tomei, 2006). If you have, therefore, a sense that you are busier than before *because* of technology, then it's likely to be true. For every new piece of technology introduced to the classroom or teaching environment, we need to learn it, communicate with students about it, be aware of updates, and so on.

58   *What's your time thief?*

Chapter 4 activity - technology

Reflect on your relationship with technology.

1   Are you more like Kevin or Huiling? If you are more like Kevin, list the reasons you are resistant to engaging with technology (be honest).
2   What technology do you engage with the most each day? If it's simple, like Microsoft Word, do you invest in learning how to use it at an advanced level? If not, why not?
3   Would you be more prepared to use technology if you had more time to learn about platforms?

Chapter 4 summary and activities

In this chapter, we've explored those issues that emerge as the most common when it comes to academics feeling 'out of control'. If you have not completed any of the activities in the chapter, but some of the issues raised feel familiar, I recommend you go back and reflect on your current thoughts and practice. This will provide a baseline against which you can measure your progress in the longer term.

The next chapter will aim to help us move forward by examining strategies to help us gain control of our time.

References and further reading

Social media

For more on social media:

Cosco, T. D. (2015). Medical journals, impact and social media: An ecological study of the Twitter-sphere. *CMAJ, 187*(18), 1353-1357. doi:10.1503/cmaj.150976
Mohammadi, E., Thelwall, M., Kwasny, M., & Holmes, K. L. (2018). Academic information on Twitter: A user survey. *PLoS One, 13*(5), e0197265. doi:10.1371/journal.pone.0197265
Tonia, T., Van Oyen, H., Berger, A., Schindler, C., & Künzli, N. (2016). If I tweet will you cite? The effect of social media exposure of articles on downloads and citations. *International Journal of Public Health, 61*(4), 513-520. doi:10.1007/s00038-016-0831-y

The two articles mentioned in this chapter were:

Egan, G. (2016, August 26). Why academics should NOT make time for social media. *Times Higher Education (Online)*. Retrieved from www.timeshighereducation.com/blog/why-academics-should-not-make-time-social-media
Miah, A. (2016, August 18). Why academics should make time for social media. *Times Higher Education* (Online). Retrieved from www.timeshighereducation.com/comment/why-academics-should-make-time-for-social-media-app

Technology

There's now an increasing body of research to support the use of augmented and virtual reality in the classroom. The simplest reason for success is that it increases the sense of authenticity or 'reality' of learning. See https://edtechmagazine.com/k12/article/2019/03/k-12-teachers-use-augmented-and-virtual-reality-platforms-teach-biology-perfcon. However, we know that technology in the classroom adds to workload. See, as examples:

Acton, R. D., Chipman, J. G., Lunden, M., & Schmitz, C. C. (2015). Unanticipated teaching demands rise with simulation training: Strategies for managing faculty workload. *Journal of Surgical Education*, *72*(3), 522–529. doi:10.1016/j.jsurg.2014.10.013

Tomei, L. A. (2006). The impact of online teaching on faculty load: Computing the ideal class size for online courses. *Journal of Technology & Teacher Education*, *14*(3), 531–541.

Tomei, L. A., & Nelson, D. (2019). The impact of online teaching on faculty load – revisited: Computing the ideal class size for traditional, online, and hybrid courses. *International Journal of Online Pedagogy and Course Design (IJOPCD)*, *9*(3), 1–12. doi:10.4018/ijopcd.2019070101

5 Controlling the time thief

Before we can invert the tornado, whereby we maximise the impact of our effort, we need to learn how to manage life on the treadmill. Under the assumption that it is never going to stop, our challenge is to learn to control the speed, and/or be adept at leaping off and leaping back on seamlessly to give ourselves a break or time to catch up and refocus.

Everything in this chapter is written with full appreciation of some of the issues associated with casualisation and stress in the workload. Nothing is suggested as an excuse - these are simply examples for consideration as we negotiate difficult terrain. I will also reinforce some of the points made in the previous chapter, so if you feel like you're reading it again, it's because I felt the issue was important enough to re-state.

Developing a 'treadmill routine'

If you've ever done a treadmill workout, one of the useful skills to learn is how to leap off the moving rubber mat onto the sides with both feet while the treadmill is still in motion to give yourself a short break. When you're ready, you lift yourself back down onto the moving band to continue at speed. This allows you to maintain momentum while also taking deliberate breaks that allow you to catch your breath, take a sip of water, or adjust your music, before you get back on the treadmill band to keep going. You must be careful, though - if you don't think about that moment you jump off the band, you can fall.

The previous chapter identified many issues, all of which ultimately affect academic time, efficiency, and efficacy. This chapter will focus on those that, in my view, make the most impact as we attempt to contain our time. Some of the issues identified in Chapter 4 won't be addressed here. Rather, we'll talk about them in our next chapter wherein we explore maximising effectiveness. Wasted opportunities, for example, are not necessarily time control issues, but related to overall efficacy - what I call 'inverting the tornado' - so we're doing less for greater impact.

When working with money, we can only spend what we have, unless we access credit. That's what we do with time. We spend what we don't have in the form of 'work seep' and sleep deprivation. This chapter accepts that you should have no extra time to give. You should know exactly what time you have, because you will have assessed this in

Chapter 2. Work seep should therefore be minimalised. With the exception of short intensive bursts such as a marking block, we are aiming to work to the hours (and their associated categories) we have identified as being available.

Slowing the treadmill

Ideally, we slow the treadmill so we're working at a steady pace. We can't sustain an ongoing sprint, even if we step off for a while to catch our breath.

We can slow the treadmill if we focus on reduction strategies. We want to reduce the amount of:

- email traffic generally;
- time we say the same thing twice (and more);
- marking we do;
- time we spend on marking;
- time we spend to create materials or prepare for a class that we only use once;
- time we look for stuff that should be easy to find;
- unnecessary travel we do;
- time we counsel individual students about their assessment;
- time we manage bushfires; and
- time we spend to organise meetings.

Many of the issues in the last chapter would be addressed by paying attention to these treadmill-slowing aims. We need to pose these as questions: *'How do I . . . ?'* as this will force us to act. *'We can't because . . .'* is simply not an acceptable response. If you're fixed on being unable to do anything about your circumstance, then it is time to put this book down.

How do we reduce the amount of email traffic generally?

Some academics simply reduce email by not responding to email. This might control time, but isn't effective in the long run. Students will complain, pressure will build, the inbox fills with repeated 'You haven't responded to my email' emails. It's extremely stressful. This strategy is simply ignoring the need to be on the treadmill, but eventually we'll fall off anyway.

I receive excellent satisfaction scores and overall rates of student success, yet I have strict rules about email for all students except my RhD candidates. I devised this approach in response to asking the following question: *'Why do students send emails?'*.

1 They may have not attended class when something important was discussed [Not generally my problem, unless a significant life event occurred at the time].
2 They haven't read the course profile [Not my problem].
3 They couldn't find the information [Maybe my problem].

62 Controlling the time thief

4   They have a personal issue that is affecting their study [Definitely interested, even if not my problem].
5   They have a last-minute question about the assignment, which is due in half an hour [Not my problem that they left it to the last minute].
6   They aren't getting on with their group [Maybe interested, but not specifically my problem].
7   It's easier to ask me than do the work to find the answer [Absolutely their problem].
8   Lacking confidence and seeking reassurance [Both our problems, and I have a role to play in building this, but not via email].
9   They are seeking feedback on assignments [Absolutely legitimate, but not via email].
10 They don't want to discuss their assessment in public [This is a confidence issue, and there are other ways to build this than engaging in email interaction].
11 They hate me and want to complain about me [Our collective problem, but there are still better ways to communicate than via email].

It seemed clear that enabling students by responding to them was to engage in their drama, thus making it mine. This is 'problem transferral' by students onto us (or one another). I do not believe in being rude, so 'Not my problem' is not a reason to be rude or dismissive. Simply ignoring or belittling a student is poor behaviour. There's no room for it in a classroom, however frazzled we may feel. My approach – always kind and fair, but mostly firm.

Another question arose: *'How do we become firm or set boundaries with students, without being rude or humiliating them (noting the principle that people remember the way you make them feel)?'*.

I adopted a range of strategies, some of which I will expand and build on. These are based on the principle that there will be *one source of central information*. That source of information should not be me via individual response on email.

This includes information about the course, information about assessment, feedback on assignments, and so on. If I can request that students access information that is *easy to find and in one place before* contacting me, then I can hope they will find the answer they need.

Strategies that support this include:

- **Develop a Frequently Asked Questions (FAQ) webpage associated with your course (most have online presence these days).** An alternative is to distribute an updated FAQ weekly to students via email – whatever works best for your context.
- **Update the FAQ as issues and questions arise on discussion forums and via email.** Update the FAQ first. Then respond to the student with the following:

  Thanks for your question. I have updated the FAQ with the answer, which is: [include the answer]. You can see the response here: [include link].

  It's course policy to check the FAQ before asking questions via email or the discussion forum. This means everyone gets the same information and reduces communication traffic, which is of help to us all. I hope this helps!

Controlling the time thief 63

- **Set contact hours for virtual engagement (I refer to these as virtual office hours) with students.** This is the only time I respond to students via email, phone, or discussion board. I set aside 6 hours per week under 'teaching' for this purpose. I see this as a 'virtual class' whereby I do everything related to teaching outside scheduled classes. I set my office hours (virtual and on-campus are held at the same time) in 2-hour blocks every second day: Monday mornings to cater for weekend interaction and set students up for the week, Wednesday evenings to cater for working and distance students, and Friday afternoons to close off any loose ends before the weekend.
- **Centralise communication.** Make sure everything is in one place. We tend to use lectures for this purpose generally, and then complain that students miss critical information because they don't show up. The question arises: *'How do I communicate critical information for students outside lectures?'*. You could incorporate key information into your FAQ page or send a weekly email/class newsletter. There are many ways to do this, but it is our job to make sure that information is in one place, and easy for students to find.
- **Articulate expectations on communication, including engagement in class, on online forums, and via social media.** This also includes guidelines that set expectations for last-minute questions and requests about assessment. Outline these in course orientation and refer to it repeatedly. Here's a statement I use:

  Teaching staff will not be available to respond to last-minute requests about the assignment on the day prior to or the day the assignment is due. This places undue and unreasonable pressure on us, and you will have been given plenty of opportunity to discuss assessment during the term. Requests for extension may be placed within this time, but may not be approved/responded to on the day.

- **Be confident to use the phone.** Many of my colleagues don't like doing this because a phone call can take longer than an email. I see this as an investment, particularly if I have a student agitator or someone who is asking repeated questions via email or on the discussion forum.

Students soon learn to go to the FAQ first. In my experience, I started to receive: *'It's OK, thanks I have found what I need'* emails after I started doing this. Each term, I feel busy in the first few weeks as students get to know the 'rules'. By the end of term, everything feels under control. Students in my advanced courses are familiar with my approach, which has been generally adopted by teaching peers.

The only reason I generally now engage in email interaction with a student is when they wish to raise a personal issue with me that will affect their study. I'll then usually talk to them by phone, and perhaps record the interaction via email. I still get emails, but not many as a percentage of the students in my class (say four emails in the final week of term from a class of 300).

64 *Controlling the time thief*

How do we reduce the amount of time we're saying the same thing twice (and more)?

The previous strategies - centralised communication and FAQs - will cover this. You may come up with other creative ways to achieve this, but you will be most successful if you work to the reality of human behaviour (it is likely that most students won't turn up to all lectures or watch the entire recording) as opposed to our desired behaviour (that students need to come to class or do the readings to get the information they need). If you really want to be sure that a student reads information, find a way to assess it.

How do we reduce the amount of marking we're doing?

Creating assessment, like content, is a core activity for teaching academics. I am going to assume here that readers are familiar with the need to align assessment with learning outcomes, and state that it's beyond the scope of this book to engage with the broader literature and significant body of knowledge behind designing effective learning activities and feedback strategies.

My concern is the relationship between designing assessment and the impact it then has on the time of the academic who manages that assessment.

One of the first discussions I have when working with academics concerns assessment: *'Tell me about the assessment in your course'*. I will always ask questions about how the assessment links with the learning outcomes, and about how grades are allocated. This tells me about the academic I am working with, their worldview, and their experience with pedagogy and curriculum design.

When we're on the treadmill of an academic year, we don't pay as much attention to excellent assessment design as we should. We may have the best intentions in the world, but when the time comes to write exam questions, or review the assessment for a future term, we end up 'just getting things done' without due respect for the impact this may have on our time in the future.

Poor assessment design impacts on our time in the following ways:

- Too many non-automated assessments will take time to mark.
- Too many automated assessments (online quizzes) poorly integrated (such as summative as opposed to formative) may not engage students, which could affect their ability to understand concepts deeply at advanced levels. We can find that more students seek our support as they try to complete complex tasks.
- Assessment that is not appropriately scaffolded will result in repeat problems. Thus, we will be repeating the same comments. Even with a comments bank at our fingertips, this is time consuming (and soul destroying).
- Assessment that doesn't apply an appropriate feedback model doesn't add value and we will have the same problem as the previous point (see also the next section on time spent marking).

Controlling the time thief 65

I think we don't address assessment because:

- For most of us, it doesn't happen every day or week, so it's out of sight and mind for chunks of our year.
- We view marking as an 'out of hours' activity – something we do above and beyond 'the job'.

Simple strategies to reduce marking load might include:

- group assessment (although this comes with its own issues that can add to workload);
- non-written alternatives (such as presentations);
- peer review (again, comes with limitations); and
- self-assessment (which encourages students to engage with requirements).

I will specifically talk more about some of these in Chapter 6.

How do we reduce the amount of time we're spending on marking?

We tend to see marking blocks as a chunk of time, but when I have questioned academics about exactly how much time they spend marking, they refer to a period, such as 'I have two weeks to get the assignments back to students' or 'I have three weeks to finish the exam marking'. They may leave marking until the end of a day, after attending to work in the form of student consultation, meetings, and normal classes to run.

The question to ask here is: *'Exactly how much time does it take to mark one item of assessment?'.*

The formula should be:

Number of assignments × average time per item + 20% of total (for logging in, checking plagiarism, doing a skim read before we review deeply, moderation, problem assignments)

This is the *minimum* number of hours. Once you have calculated the hours required, schedule them into your week/s, noting that these are the weeks that you can expect to work some overtime.

Scheduling marking blocks that are consistent with the *actual* time required to mark them sounds simple, but is not applied as strictly as it should be. So, to control your time better, work on scheduling your marking realistically. It was only when I did this that I really started to question my assessment practices generally – I simply had to reduce the amount of time I lost to 'tornado work'.

Some solutions are quite simple. Here's an example of a conversation I had with a new staff member when reviewing their assessment practices:

66 *Controlling the time thief*

Me: I notice that you ask students to create a PowerPoint presentation for one of the assessments, and that you give the students a grade for the design of the presentation.

Academic: That's correct.

Me: Do you teach students how to design a PowerPoint presentation within course content, or is it pre-requisite knowledge?

Academic: No, we don't specifically teach PowerPoint. I just want students to present professional work.

Me: OK, but you have three criteria in your grading sheet relating to this – written work, design of the PowerPoint, and presentation. The overall outcome of the course doesn't include any reference to being able to present professionally, but focuses on an ability to synthesise and present a clear argument.

Academic: That's correct.

Me: Do you actually care whether it's PowerPoint?

Academic: Not really. I hadn't really thought about it.

Me: So if you reduced the three criteria to one, which focuses on synthesis and argument, would that be easier to mark? You wouldn't need to provide specific feedback on the PowerPoint presentation in that case.

Academic: I suppose so.

We can over-assess and overcomplicate assessment, and fail to focus on core learning outcomes when we do assess. I use this PowerPoint example because it's come across my desk on so many occasions. When students are asked to develop a presentation, there are often marks associated with that presentation and what it looks like, or its quality. That's fine if the student is studying a visual design or communication course.

If, however, the student is studying a foundation business course, and the assessment focus is to demonstrate an ability to synthesise critical ideas, then does it matter what the presentation looks like? If you're spending time adding up marks on a crowded or long checklist, you're not only wasting time but you're asking students to waste their time, as well.

Given the number of different options now available to students, does it matter whether they use PowerPoint, Prezi, Keynote, or even PDF files? It is a different matter if students are studying an advanced level course, whereby presentations are expected to be professional and students have been progressively taught what 'professional' looks like within that particular discipline. In my experience, however, this is rare.

There are many arguments that suggest increasingly crowded curriculum. If we take the view that we should generally not assess that which we have not explicitly taught, then we are in a position to refine our practice. This will save us time.

A second question to ask to reduce the amount of time we spend marking is: *'How do I improve the quality of student submissions?'*. Better quality work will reduce the amount of time we spend providing feedback.

Developing strategies that focus on scaffolding and opportunities for formative feedback don't need to be onerous, but they do require proactive engagement and thought.

We could do any one or all of the following.

- Provide exemplars and explain them (recorded, so we don't have to do it twice).
- Ask students to self-assess (provide recorded instruction on how to do this).
- Incorporate response to feedback in assessment (require students to submit a short appendix on how they incorporated feedback from our pre-feedback sessions [which gave advice on what not to do] and from specific feedback from earlier drafts or pieces into their assignment). Including this becomes a 'requirement of the task'.
- Include a line of criteria in a rubric that assesses student ability to 'meet the requirement of the task' as an incentive to review all the requirements. This is reinforced through self-assessment, whereby students are asked to give themselves a grade on this rubric.

  Here's an example of a line of criteria in a rubric I use in a writing course (noting that I keep it quite broad and complement the rubric with a comment bank):

Attention to requirements of the task

Requirement	Fail	Pass	Credit	Distinction	High distinction
Attention to requirements of task, which includes: Required word count. Justification of intended publication, target audience, and discussion as to why the article is of interest. Transcript of interviews. List of contacts.	Submission is missing aspects of task, or task requirements have been misunderstood.	Satisfactory effort in attending to all requirements of task. Some areas could have been more detailed.	Very good effort in attending to most requirements of the task. A number of gaps evident.	Excellent effort in attending to all requirements of the task. All items demonstrate due attention with some minor gaps.	Professional effort in attending to all requirements of the task. No gaps.

Of course, not all students will take notice of exemplars, or feedback, or the rubric. But many will. If you can help students improve the quality of their work, and thus the time you spend marking, for *most* students, you will save yourself lots of time in a big course. We will talk more about self-assessment in future chapters.

68 *Controlling the time thief*

How do we reduce the amount of time we're spending on creating materials or preparing for a class?

When we're on the treadmill, it's easy to just do what is easy. We write lectures on the run or at the last minute, or record our video lectures, upload our notes, and insert readings into our online learning management system. This can create 'noise' for students – handouts, readings, links, and multiple places for them to go to get the same (or conflicting) information.

As highlighted in the example in Chapter 4 on lecture preparation, questions to ask include: *'How do I make sure I do this preparation once, so that I only need to refine and update from there?'*, and more generally: *'How do I future-proof my teaching materials?'*. Some effective strategies are:

- Invest in 'flipped classroom' style materials (videos, animated slides, flashcards, quizzes) that explain core well-established principles.
- When delivering recorded lectures, or recording a case note or discussion, avoid reference to current time. If we are delivering a lecture on a generic topic, with an example included for discussion, we should make sure the time-based reference to the example remains broad if a lecture is going to be recorded and incorporated as a resource into teaching materials.
- If we need all students to watch a video or review a resource, or think this will assist students, embed it into assessment.
- Design classes so they are student-centred, and reward student effort via assessment.

Taking a student-centred approach that focuses on assessment can transfer time liability from us to students, but we need to consider time on task for the student, and ensure that it's effective and aligned assessment. We can either spend hours writing lectures, or design our classes in such a way to encourage students to do the thinking. For example, I can either deliver a lecture on Benjamin Franklin the journalist, or I can ask students to conduct targeted research in class that answers a few key questions about Benjamin Franklin. Students will turn up if it's assessable, and better still, they have had a say in the way the class is taught.

How do we reduce the amount of time we're looking for stuff that should be easy to find?

There are so many ways to organise information these days, it's impossible to mention them all. There's no right answer to the question: *'What is the best way to organise my information so it's easier to find?'*. Everyone is different, and our brains are differently organised. All I can say here is that if we spend any more than 5 minutes looking for anything at one time, we need to come up with a system – by category, date, person, or whatever works. Our schedule will remind us that we don't have the time to waste on unnecessary 'fluff', such as finding a file, reading, name, or contact.

Controlling the time thief 69

Information that should be really easy to find includes:

- Evidence that we can use, such as student feedback, peer review, or student results at the end of term that indicate an improvement. Find a way to file this and annotate what it means at the time, and the impact it makes. It will save *hours* when the time comes for tenure, promotion, teaching awards, or grant applications.
- Research articles, by key word. It doesn't matter whether we use EndNote, Mendeley, or Zotero. Just use one, and spend the time to know how to use it properly.

I use categories in email so that I block like emails together – any student-related emails, for example, are categorised 'Student', and I only attend to them during virtual office hours unless urgent. I archive them in more specific folders (Teaching > Course Name > Term) so I can keep specific records. Everyone will have different approaches, and any that work under the *'How do I find it within a minute?'* rule are appropriate for email. If we can't, then we should spend some time on developing a system.

How do we reduce the amount of unnecessary travel we do?

This problem was highlighted in Chapter 4. I reinforce it here because it's one of those areas many of us are 'torn' about, and making firm decisions about my travel made a positive impact on my career. With a fixed schedule, you will be able to identify how much time you lose to travel. Taking three or four days out of a week might be workable every few months, but any more than this and it is worth questioning the value of travel against the time lost.

I restrict conferences to one or two a year, as a general rule. I always make sure the paper is written and submitted or ready for submission prior to presentation. I am increasingly looking for the ability to present online when invited to speak or present somewhere.

I need to travel a lot for work, but try to restrict it to 'overnights' when I can, whereby I drop children at school in the morning, head for an airport, spend one night away, and return the next evening. This enables me to fulfil whatever commitment I have, but reduces the amount of time I am 'perceived' to be away by my family.

Reflect on your responses to questions posed in Chapter 4's travel activity. A summary question is simply: *'Why am I travelling, and what's the personal cost of being away from home/workplace?'*. The two specific strategies I implemented that helped me were to:

- Pick a firm number of conferences I will attend (say two a year) and stick to that figure. This means I can relax and delete most conference invitations that come across my desk. Of course, there are always exceptions for that perfectly targeted conference, but this becomes the exception rather than the rule.
- Devote my attention to 'calls for papers' or journal articles – it is these that I will present at conferences, usually after they have been submitted, or while they are under review.

70 *Controlling the time thief*

How do we reduce the amount of time we're counselling individual students about their assessment?

Providing feedback to students is important, but individual student counselling can be contained. The reasons students seek specific guidance from faculty are that they:

- lack confidence (doing it for them, or over-supporting them, will not build this);
- lack skills (are we the only person in the world who can provide them with the skill they are lacking?); and
- want reassurance (they will get this when they achieve results beyond their expectations).

High-achieving students are often those who seek individual attention, as they fear failure so want to 'check' that they are on the right track. However, if we spend all our time with a student who is going to achieve well anyway, how are we looking after those who do need our help but are possibly more reluctant to seek it?

Developing a support structure for those who won't come to us will help to contain counselling requirements. Examples include:

- automated formative assessments whereby students can test themselves before submission;
- video-based pre-feedback sessions that students are required to address as part of their submission (as discussed earlier);
- peer feedback, whereby peers provide feedback to one another based on an established set of 'what to look for' guidelines (feedback rules, politeness conventions, and lessons on how to give feedback constructively are important here);
- exemplars that provide an overview of what is required, and explanations of results given to pre-inform students;
- class-based presentations on ideas or structure to receive real-time feedback; and
- public drafting, whereby student drafts are only reviewed publicly (in class, via computer) or online (via discussion forums) in a safe-fail environment.

I reduced private requests for drafts specifically by focusing on the last point. I only review drafts publicly (in class) or online (I have a separate discussion board dedicated to student drafts). All students can submit a draft, but I have rules about time limits (no less than a week prior to submission, as an example). Routinely, only three or four students in a class of 40 (roughly 10%) will submit an online draft. I will respond during my contact hours to these students. I frame this as follows:

> *I review drafts but only those submitted online or prior to class for discussion in class. This is so all students benefit from my feedback – very often, there are common themes for improvement. I know this can be confronting, but comments will be constructive and positive. Comments will be general in nature, indicating whether you are on the right track, and may have specific points to consider that will assist*

the broader class. Feedback from previous terms has reinforced that this approach works, and impacts positively on class grades overall. Please ensure you review the drafts and my feedback in the event that you are unable or unwilling to submit a draft.

Some of my colleagues are concerned about copying and privacy. These may be valid concerns, depending on context. In my classes, public drafting is always optional, but caters in particular to those high-achieving students seeking feedback. I could refuse to review drafts at all, but the time I spend reviewing drafts (maybe a few hours per term) pays off when I get the bulk of assignments and see that many students clearly took notice of the feedback.

My assessment is also heavily scaffolded – the idea being that by the end of the session, students should feel like everything's quite easy. In fact, my course design aims to peak student load and discomfort about the Week 9 or 10 mark of term – unfortunately always when the satisfaction surveys are released, and students are not liking me very much for making them work so hard!

How do I reduce the amount of time I'm putting out bushfires?

In academic contexts, bushfires become tornadoes and power treadmills. Bushfires occur most easily when the conditions are suitable. These conditions might include:

- slow response times by academic staff (and no clear explanation of when response might occur);
- inconsistent advice by teaching staff (addressed by clear guidance to the teaching team);
- materials not updated, inconsistent information provided, or information is factually incorrect;
- poor teaching quality (boring lectures, poorly organised class, teachers not turning up);
- dismissive or rude behaviour by staff; and/or
- limited feedback associated with low grades.

All these things lead to dissatisfied students who become easily agitated, and rightly so. Agitation spreads quickly when students get together – in class, via social media, or via class-based discussion forums if studying online.

Chapter 4 asked you to reflect on an instance of a bushfire. When it comes to moving forward and taking preventative steps, we can ask two summary questions to define our action: *'How do I prevent a bushfire?'*, and *'How do I contain a bushfire?'*.

I became a better teacher and administrator by focusing on the first question. We can prevent bushfires by setting expectations, and then meeting them. We should communicate with our teaching teams so we are all on the same page. We can develop materials so they are easily updated, applying simple techniques like avoiding reference

72 *Controlling the time thief*

to page numbers in textbooks (which can change when the text is updated) and developing a checklist to make sure information about assessment for due dates is consistent between course outlines and learning management submissions. The list is long. We can rethink our approach to lectures and classes, basing our practice on the premise that every hour we are all in class (including students) is an hour we don't get back. We need to make it worth the effort.

The points about dismissive or rude behaviour and limited feedback are the easiest to fix. Taking an empathy-based perspective, we simply need to imagine ourselves at the receiving end of our behaviour or feedback. It doesn't matter how stupid, rude, or ignorant we think our students might be; we must be kind in our language and provide guidance in our practice.

If a bushfire starts regardless of our efforts, then we need to contain it and contain it early. To contain it early, we need to be aware that it's happening. This means monitoring social media, and discussion forums (in our contact hours). I also make personal contact with student agitators – that is, a student who is continually asking questions and looking for fault. I will either phone them or meet them personally, and then record that conversation for filing. The principle behind this is 'keep your enemies close' but in many cases, it's simply that the student wants to be heard. It provides us the opportunity to explain our approach and rationale if they are complaining. If we are disorganised and the term is a train wreck, it is hard to apologise, but we can give the student an opportunity to air any specific issues which may prevent their flames from spreading.

Setting our own pace on the treadmill

Setting our own pace is particularly difficult, especially for casual, sessional, and junior academic staff. All of us are, to some extent, running on other people's treadmills. The extent to which we allow ourselves to be affected by other people is very contextual. I'll refer back to the academic types in Chapter 1 – some of us, like 'preppers', get swept onto a systemic treadmill, while others, like 'project-focused academics', simply stand on the side. I have heard many peers lament the lack of control they perceive they have on their workload.

In addition to some of the ideas presented so far, the two ways we can act to influence our pace on the treadmill are:

- communicate clearly about our limits and expectations, and
- stay focused on *our* story.

Identify and communicate our limits and expectations clearly

We must have clarity of thought to communicate clearly. If we aren't clear about our boundaries, or our requirements, therefore, we can't communicate them.

Brian is the Goth Studies PhD student we met in the previous chapter who was caught up on his supervisor Jane's treadmill. We identified that Brian was affected by Jane's

Controlling the time thief 73

approach to student communication whereby she was over-responsive and thus generating work for Brian. This case provides an opportunity to illustrate; while Brian can't control Jane, he could do the following:

- have a conversation with Jane about consistent email policies in courses he teaches;
- request that Jane create and update a FAQ online page that students are required to review prior to asking routine questions from teaching staff (if Jane doesn't, Brian might create one for his class);
- request that Jane develop office contact hours for student email and discussion forum communication three times per week (he could then request his students check any forum messages prior to contacting him);
- set class rules that explain his position in terms of hours available to teach students; and
- create class-based peer groups, whereby students are required to communicate with their peers before contacting him if they are unclear about something (students could nominate one person contact him out of class if any points of clarification are required).

Jane might refuse to get organised. Jane might also get upset or feel pressured that Brian is making unreasonable requests. Jane might decide that she won't use Brian again as a tutor in her course. However, Brian is well-liked by students and receives good results. Replacing him would add to her workload because she would need to orient a new tutor. Ultimately, however, if Brian contains his time even by an hour or two a week, it's time he gets back to complete his PhD. This is more important to him in the long term.

The benefit of identifying time available in our fixed schedule is that we realise, in concrete terms, our limits. We have a reason to say no, but can present options when potentially rejecting an offer: 'I can't give you five hours a week, but I can give you half an hour'; 'I can't review that paper this month, but can do it next month'; 'I can take on an extra class next term, but this term I'm at my limit'; 'I think your proposal is really interesting, but can't take on any more PhD students at the moment. I recommend you contact X'.

We might struggle with this as a 'newbie' but we do get better at this as we become more experienced.

Stay focused on our story

Some of us don't know what we want our academic story to be. We know we want to be an academic, but that's about it. It's easy, when we haven't identified our personal and academic narrative, to get drawn into other people's treadmills – their projects, their dramas, their priorities.

Our challenge is to ensure that whatever choice we make about work we do, where we have a choice, it is contributing positively to our overall narrative.

74 *Controlling the time thief*

It took me a long time to be able to do this. I was assisted by a fantastic mentor who was brave enough to tell me how frustrated she was at the way I chased ideas and jumped around. She asked: 'What's your narrative going to be?'. At the time, I was bouncing around from project to project. Her question prompted me to more firmly align decisions with a broader picture of what I wanted to be known for as an academic. I came up with a definition of myself. If I am not able to align anything I do with improving my knowledge of education, regional communities, or community storytelling and communication in the public sphere, I am not available to engage.

If you don't know what your story is, complete the projection activity in the next section.

Chapter 5 summary and activities

In this chapter, we've identified ways to control your time. Many build on the scenarios in Chapter 4. Some of these are very basic, like clearly communicating your availability. Others require you to examine your approach to course organisation.

The next chapter will aim to help us move forward, by examining specific strategies to maximise the effect of single effort – what I call inverting the tornado.

Chapter 5 activity 1 – controlling the treadmill

Of the topics and strategies mentioned in this chapter, which is the most applicable to you and can you take action to improve your practice? Record your response in detail – identify what the problem is, why you think it is a problem, what you are going to do to amend your practice, and what you hope this will achieve.

Chapter 5 activity 2 – projection: your story

If you find yourself jumping around from idea to idea, developing a more focused approach will help you make decisions, and consequently contain your time. This activity simply asks you to project beyond simply wanting tenure or promotion.

Write a short paragraph that builds on the following:

> At the age of 60, I will be known for my work in <insert area of interest/focus>, <insert area of interest/focus>, and <insert area of interest/focus>. I will be known as an excellent and organised teacher who is well known for <whatever you might want to be known for in your teaching>.

You may need to workshop this to come up with your areas of focus. Things can change, but asking the question, *'How is this decision helping me achieve what I want to be known for?'* will inform your decisions when considering how to spend your time.

6 Inverting the tornado

Having achieved some order on our treadmill, we now want to achieve impact with less 'spin', whereby we 'invert' the tornado. This means we maximise the impact of an hour of our time. The focus is on teaching, with the overall intent being to improve student experience and results. This will reduce the potential for bushfires, and free up time for scholarship, research, or professional development – whatever we want to be doing with our time.

The question that drives my practice is: *'How do we invert our effort so that we are helping those that need it, helping others who care to some extent, but not bending over backwards for those who are making calculated decisions about their study and trying to get through without effort or pushing others to make the effort for them?'*.

In this chapter, we move from controlling our time on the treadmill to inverting the tornado – doing things smarter so that our spin is minimised, and our impact is maximised. This usually means combining elements of our practice – not doing one thing differently, as we might when trying to contain time, but doing many things differently in complementary ways. It also requires an investment of time early or at critical periods.

The three areas I am going to focus on are attitude and engagement, communication, and making effort count. Again, some of these concepts will be feeling very familiar as we build on ideas and strategies introduced in previous chapters.

Attitude and engagement

Our attitude to teaching depends on our worldview and is aligned to our academic type and stage of career. The 'sage on the stage' has been replaced by student-centred learning, and students are coming to college or university far more literate and diverse in their knowledge about technology, decision-making, and learning techniques. Even if they don't know what's good for them, they think they do. Students may think they can absorb information at a glance, they may think it's appropriate to use the same language they use to text friends in an academic piece of work, and they may think that we are their personal coaches after years of being coached at high school by teachers in preparation for success to get into college.

76 Inverting the tornado

If it is particularly important to us, we need to make it important to students. And what is important to students is achievement - manifested through assessment and results.

Let's explore an example.

Kevin is our biology professor (he has recovered from his heart attack). He teaches very traditionally. Each week, he delivers a 2-hour lecture, and students are required to participate in one lab and a workshop. Online students are required to participate in a residential school during term break. Assessment in the course comprises:

- *one written report - 20% (30 minutes each to mark);*
- *two online quizzes - 15% (automatically marked, including feedback); and*
- *one formal examination - 50% (30 minutes each to mark).*

Kevin prepares and delivers lectures, some of which are based on the textbook. He does spend time updating his lectures to cater for latest developments. For example, three weeks were recently devoted to the most dangerous organisms, whereby he spent the lecture hours providing examples of dangerous bacteria and their characteristics. Students complain that Kevin is boring and that some of the materials are outdated. They say he reads his lecture notes, and they aren't sure about the relevance of some of the material. Kevin notes that many students in class are on their laptops. He isn't sure whether they are doing legitimate research or whether they are surfing social media. He spends a lot of time fielding questions from students about what was missed in lectures and seeking explanation about facts. The overall pass rate of the course is around 70%, and the attrition rate is high. Overall, there is no real need to change, but room for improvement and increasing pressure to increase the pass rate.

This remains a very common approach to 'teaching'. It's easy and safe. However, the students aren't as engaged as they could be, and Kevin needs to repeat a lot of information. He fields a lot of consultation requests for coaching and examination preparation. Let's look at an alternative:

Kevin reduces his lecture time from 2 hours to 1 hour per week. Students are required to attend workshops and deliver group presentations on key topics or participate in peer review. Students elect the topic on which they wish to work, and are required to teach the class for that week/session. Students must attend class to provide feedback to their peers, guided by established answers to questions posed. Students are assured that all questions will be addressed in some way in the exam. Online students work virtually and deliver presentations when they attend residential schools.
Assessment is now:

- *group presentation/individual report (including self-assessment and peer review) - 50% (30 minutes each to mark); and*
- *examination - 50% (30 minutes each to mark).*

Automatically marked online quizzes are no longer compulsory, but encouraged as formative assessment. Students may repeat the online quizzes as many times as they like, and detailed feedback is provided on all answers. Students are provided with a rationale for the approach. Clear guidelines are developed around presentation requirements, including questions they must address, and group work. The assessment rubric includes a statement on working together, and students are reminded that when they work in labs, they will always be required to work as a team.

Kevin feels nervous, because he has normally prepared a 2-hour lecture. He is also nervous about the standard of presentations, and about whether students will do the work required. At the end of term, however, he is surprised by the quality of presentations, feels he has learned some new information from the students, and tutors report that most students have turned up to class each week.

On initial review, this alternative scenario seems messier and potentially more problematic. It would certainly be the case if you didn't have clear class rules. However, it is very student-centric and engages the students in their learning. It ultimately becomes very 'light-touch' for teaching staff after the initial orientation to requirements. Students will attend class because everything they are doing is assessed – from presenting to reviewing students. Those who don't attend class are making calculated decisions about the level to which they seek to pass the course. This alternative approach reflects a successful intervention in one of my courses some years ago (see Ames, 2016).

While initially more effort was required to set up the assessment topics and create rubrics, peer review guidelines, and so on, students engaged with one another and the materials once term started and appeared motivated to research. In the preceding scenario, Kevin saved prep/walking across campus time (around 2 hours per week, totalling 28 hours in a 14-week term). Kevin may need to spend time (say 4 hours) to create orientation materials for the assessment, but he only needs to do this once if he is teaching in repeat terms. He will spend a few hours setting up the groups for group work, and may field some questions during term. Overall, though, he's saving time in real terms. It required him to change his worldview and adapt his practice.

Obviously, this is an illustrative example, and there are *many* different factors at play when we make decisions about our approach – institutional rules about student contact hours, policies on assessment and exams, and staff responsibilities, as examples – but rethinking assessment design and delivery in terms of real hours available is a worthwhile activity. Perception of how long something will take us often does not equal reality.

In all cases, students should be required to self-assess against an assessment rubric. This reduces the potential for them to 'miss something', and encourages them to engage in the requirements of the task. This in turn requires us to ensure that those requirements are clear to students. Students will also push back on group work, particularly high-achieving students who often complain that they are doing all the work. In many cases, this might be true but those students may elect to do all the work because they want higher grades. As an example of the way I try to encourage critical reflection by

78 *Inverting the tornado*

students who were tempted to complain about more trivial matters (such as 'it's not fair that I have to do all the work'), I developed the following criteria for a rubric. This addressed group work and aimed to encourage students to attempt to resolve their issues internally:

Group work					
Criteria element	Fail	Pass	Credit	Distinction	High distinction
Group work	Group failed to collaborate effectively, conflict was not managed effectively, and teaching staff were required to intervene.	Group collaborated basically well, and managed conflict with minimal intervention or attention by teaching staff.	Group collaborated well, and managed conflict with no teaching staff intervention required. Some issues evident.	Group collaborated well, and managed conflict with no teaching staff intervention required. Minor issues evident.	Excellent group work. Cohesive and collaborative, and conflict was managed effectively without the need for teaching staff to get involved.

Innovative approaches will only work if they are underpinned by very clear guidelines about expectations. See the 'References and further reading' section in this chapter for more on this as a real story. In my experience, not only did overall satisfaction improve (eventually), but results improved, as well. My overall effort was less in terms of hours required to 'teach' and the overall performance of students improved.

Communication

Inverting the communication tornado is based on three interacting principles:

- be nice and/or kind;
- speak once to a crowd; and
- find opportunities to notice students.

Be nice

Academics can be mean - genuinely mean, condescending, and rude. Some academic environments are beyond toxic. I am repeatedly stunned by the impact of poor communication on academic time. Emails with no salutations, poor tone, no email at all, staff humiliating or belittling a student in class, or ignoring them on discussion boards; all of these set conditions for a bushfire.

We may think we are the smartest person in the room. Ideally, we should be the smartest person 'on our topic' in the room; indeed, we may be the most knowledgeable person in the world on our topic if we have a PhD and a research track record behind us. Arrogance

Inverting the tornado 79

might get us somewhere in the short term, but in the longer term, it's destructive. Our students may be disorganised, attention seeking, rude, technologically illiterate, and linguistically challenged. They may try to make their problems our problems because they may have never been challenged, or they have relied on others all their life. Maybe they need to learn how to study, or are overly anxious about their grades because of familial pressure on them to perform. We may not know what is going on in their lives.

I say this with certainty because I have routinely provided opportunities for students to tell me their stories in my classes. From writing a maiden speech to parliament that outlines their key passions and dreams for themselves and their communities, to a personal feature story or news issue, I often find myself in tears or completely stunned at the stories that are forthcoming. Stories of familial domestic violence, poverty, adventure, misadventure, disease, disability. Even students from more privileged backgrounds tell stories of having to fend for themselves from an early age because both parents worked, of the impact of functional alcoholism behind closed doors, and of pressure to achieve 'because of the amount of money we've spent on your education'. Every term, every time.

Many years ago, before I knew better, I wrote that it was an insult to receive a piece of assessment in my comments to a student in assignment feedback. I believed this to be true. Reviewing the assessment was a waste of my time and energy. I couldn't believe that the student had bothered to submit the assessment. At the time I was a working editor and tutoring communication students part-time while also studying. My time and effort was precious, and the student hadn't bothered to come to class for some weeks prior to the assignment submission.

After receiving my feedback, the student contacted me by email. Their mother had been dying. The student advised me that contacting me regarding their assessment at the time was the last thing on their mind. They had not wanted to make a fuss or ask for an extension because they were still immersed in trauma. The student had put the assignment in knowing they would fail the piece but hoping they would pass the course. That was indeed the case. A deliberate, considered act. No emails, no fuss, no making things my problem – just making a choice about what was important to them at the time. The student's email was short and sharp, but polite. I can still feel how ashamed I felt about what I had written as I learned about what had been going on in that student's life at the time of assessment.

This was one of my 'teacher-changing' moments. It reminded me that I need not take student work personally. I just needed to fail the student against the assessment criteria – no smart comments needed. Always fair, sometimes firm. I have since always respected decisions students make about their assignments.

Changing my attitude changed my language. The excuse 'I am too busy to be polite' became unacceptable. I learned that simple kindness doesn't cost much, time-wise, but saves time in the longer term. I learned that being kind doesn't mean responding immediately to every email – in fact, building resilience and self-sufficiency can be an act of kindness with appropriate explanation. Students remember the way we make them feel; they can become our advocates if we are considerate, and understand if we are firm.

80 *Inverting the tornado*

If we are rude, however, the chance of kickback or complaint increases, as does the potential for complaint cancer to spread. We do not need to be so nice that students become dependent on us. Being kind in our language does not mean we have to accept poor behaviour by a student. We can firmly, but politely, remind students of appropriate tones of communication. If a student is rude enough for us to register a complaint of assault or misconduct, take action.

My rules for student communication are:

- Address every student by their (correct) name in email communication when we can. If they don't provide their name, request that they provide it to us in communication next time.
- Don't poke the bear. Students may be rude to us. Be nicer back. This does not mean we have to give in. We can call anyone out on rude behaviour, but do it politely and in person (asking questions about reasons for their behaviour is an effective strategy, in my experience).
- When the matter is complicated, make a personal phone call, followed by writing a record of conversation.
- Avoid being arrogant; rather, be respectful. We may think the question is stupid, may be frustrated that the student clearly wasn't listening when we answered the same question a minute ago, or think the student needs a lesson in humility in front of the rest of the class. Be the bigger person.
- Don't call someone out on their behaviour in public, as a normal rule (noting that there are rare exceptions). We don't like to be called out in public - we shouldn't do it to others.
- Have a conversation with the student after class, or by phone if the student is studying online, if that student is a repeat offender on a matter that we find irritating.

These practices aren't simply related to controlling time. They invert tornadoes because if we are kind and constructive, students may communicate our rationale and be supportive of us to others and extinguish bushfires on our behalf.

Speak once to a crowd

We can't make a student come to class, but we don't want to repeat what we said in class for students who don't turn up. We don't want to receive emails from students before class who are concerned about what they will miss in class if they don't attend - they are hedging bets about what is important to them when they do this. Our time's important, and their choice to turn up is their choice. I touched on this in early chapters. In most cases, students tend to be very accepting of their responsibility if we are fair, open, transparent, and consistent. There will always be an exception, but we can reduce the number of these.

Actions that assist you to 'speak once to a crowd' build on strategies outlined in Chapter 5 when we were discussing ways to control email. They include centralising

Inverting the tornado 81

communication, creating an online FAQ list, and setting contact hours for online students. They also encourage setting rules for online engagement, and developing exemplars. Specific steps could look like the following:

- Step 1: Create an FAQ for your course.
- Step 2: Make it clear to all students, on-campus and distance, that there are virtual office (or contact) hours. This is when staff will respond to emails *and* discussion forum posts. Publicise these and don't leave too much time between blocks. (I recommend that this time be the same as face-to-face contact hours. That means that if no-one turns up, time can be devoted to interacting with online students, returning phone calls, and responding to forum posts and emails. I am sometimes quite busy with phone calls, and sometimes I'm still responding after my contact period has finished, but my goal is generally to clear the inbox by the end of the office hour period.)
- Step 3: As per the example in Chapter 5, create a standardised (yet personal) response for students who send direct emails that is polite, respectful, and reminds students of policies, but also answers their question (which you cut and paste from, or create a new response to add to, the FAQ). Send this response during designated virtual office hours.
- Step 4: Spend time developing exemplars, providing general 'what we are looking for' responses or pre-feedback recordings or emails.
- Step 5: Communicate or summarise all issues and set direction for a week/session in one place, such as via email, recorded message distributed via YouTube, or whatever's best for your context.

Peers tell me they find this difficult. It took me a while to develop a holistic approach. I was inspired when students told me they appreciated knowing when they would receive a response from me. They were able to plan, knowing that I would be online at a particular time, or they could check emails after my virtual office hour periods knowing they would have received a response. As a teacher of online and on-campus students, I can provide an outline of my practice.

As noted already, I set six hours per week aside as virtual office hours. I communicate with students during these periods – as if I were in class. I advise these times to students, and they know that if they send me an email or post on the forum during these times, it is the only time they will get an instant response.

On Mondays, I send an email or post a 'What's happening this week/Where you should be up to' overview on the discussion forum. All students, on-campus and online, and tutors are expected to read this.

I categorise any student-related email received during a normal day as 'Student'. Unless the matter is particularly urgent, I refrain from response. During my contact hours, I respond to online forum posts first. I update the FAQ list if there are some common questions. I then work through emails. If the same question is asked by email (students seem to send questions to multiple places when they're panicking), I point them to

82 *Inverting the tornado*

the online response or FAQ. If the question is assessment related, I will ask them to ask the question on the forum so that all students can benefit from my response.

I make it clear that during assessment weeks, I will not be available the day before the assignment is due to respond to last-minute questions. I am open about the amount of stress it causes me, and take a 'Your panic should not be my panic' approach. The regularity with which students accept and acknowledge this as being reasonable amazes me. I stay offline on these days. To be honest, I find the final days before a major assessment task now very quiet, even in very large classes.

This approach appears to build collegiality, resilience, and independence. In the absence of receiving an immediate response, students will turn to their peers, or do more research. My online students, for example, will assist one another, often reminding others of my hours: 'Kate won't respond to this until she is online tomorrow, but this is what I think . . .'. I will make sure I acknowledge any effort to help a student and either confirm or correct the response, but also make it clear in my course outlines that wasting online time with 'thanks'/'that's great' posts can be unnecessary.

Speaking once to a crowd also works for our teaching team if we are course coordinators. Tutor turnover is undesirable, because every time someone new joins the team, we need to orient them to content and assessment. Happy casuals who feel supported and mentored are valuable. More importantly, working with a teaching team in a large course whereby everyone works collaboratively and is familiar with the material, including sessional staff, is a rewarding experience.

Find opportunities for personal moments

The third point for communication is to find personal moments. It's very easy for students to go unnoticed – both good students and poor students. In large classes, they disappear into crowds, and maybe they don't turn up to class. Online, they lurk and work through materials, only to submit assignments and graduate having never met anyone in class. Personalising student engagement doesn't have to be time consuming. It is applicable when providing feedback and engaging difficult students.

Personalising feedback

It is quicker to speak something than it is to write it, as a rule. When considering how we might give feedback to students, audio feedback (whereby we have a personal conversation with a student about the work submitted) provides a more efficient way of responding to student work. It can also be more effective (see more on this in Chapter 7). It requires markers to engage with student work personally, proves to the student that their work was in fact read, and creates a sense of 'recognition' with a student. We can review assignments with students in class, but to do so, have to take ourselves back to their particular piece and remind ourselves what they wrote. Audio feedback can clarify student questions immediately – they can seek further information if required, but in my experience, this rarely happens. For distance students, this conversation reduces the

Inverting the tornado   83

sense of isolation – we feel that we are talking to them, and they get a sense that they are being directly addressed.

> **Example of practice:** *I use audio feedback to explain my response to student writing in feature, speech, and news writing classes. When providing audio feedback, I review the assessment, make a few notes and comment on the rubric (noting that it has been self-assessed by the student, so there's a starting point for the comment).*
> *I record a short (3–5-minute) audio file. You might use the embedded recording option in your learning management system, but I generally find it easier to use my computer microphone/record button so I don't have to be online when I'm marking. I save the file using the student's surname, and upload it to the learning management system with the rubric. I address the student by name, find something good to say about the assignment (even if it's that you're thankful the student managed to submit the piece in a busy term), and focus on what they can do to improve. This also works for students who are hearing impaired, as they can convert the speech to text via an app or conversion software.*

This effort to personalise can be efficient and effective (some of you may already do this and will be aware of how effective it is). In my case, where I might have spent 30 minutes providing written feedback on a feature article, I now spend 10 minutes completing the rubric, another 5 minutes recording my response, and 5 minutes uploading and finalising the grade. It might only save 10 minutes, but the feedback is rich. Ten minutes over 60 students is 600 minutes – or 10 hours. Importantly, the feedback has impact.

There are many other ways to provide personal feedback to students. This is the one that is most effective from a time-saving perspective, in my view.

Personal contact with 'difficult' students

Investing time to engage students who might 'set the cat among the pigeons' in your class can be tornado-inverting. These students may be overly critical of our approach, disagree with us or other students, or are over-anxious and seek explanation on very minor points that take our time away from broader or more important discussion. Proactive engagement with the student to recognise their concerns ('I noticed that you are asking a lot of questions about . . .'; 'I noticed you have been expressing your concern about . . .') can be made via a 10-minute phone call if the student is studying online, or by request for a student to stay after class, or make an appointment, to discuss their issues.

> **Illustrative example:** *I routinely teach first-in-family, mature age students studying online. Some students are not working and have a lot of time to devote to study (Student X), as opposed to peers who are working full-time and only direct attention to their study once a week (Student Y). By the time Student Y logs in to the course discussion forum on a Friday, Student X has posted 14 specific questions about assessment and picked up inconsistencies in the course coordinator's responses.*

84 *Inverting the tornado*

> *Student Y is getting frustrated because they don't want their inbox blocked with argument and silly questions. This situation would be resolved by the FAQ, and a phone call to Student X to direct them to the FAQs, to address any issues. I have had one occasion when a 20-minute phone call to a particular Student X every fortnight probably saved me an hour per week of responding to minutiae. Student X was trying to learn, by distance, a new social media platform that other students were finding quite straightforward. Student X was anxious and trying to succeed. Student X became an advocate of mine, and by the end of term was actively defending me (my courses are known for being quite confronting).*

Make a detailed record of conversation, but essentially, the purpose of the communication might be to ask the student what they suggest you do to address the issue, or to discuss all the issues they might be having. Simply allow them the voice or audience they think they need at the time. Follow this up with an email that politely explains your stance if you decide to hold firm on an issue. Don't engage in an argument. We may need to engage in some interpersonal training to do this if we have difficulty communicating, or become anxious when having difficult conversations.

There are many other strategies but these two – personalising our approach to feedback and making personal contact with 'difficult' students – are the most effective, in my experience.

Making effort count (for us and students)

Students are very astute. Most will focus on core requirements that will assist them to pass a course. A minority will be willing to engage in extension activities. Some won't bother with much, but still expect to pass.

Design for core requirements

Many of us design our courses on the premise that *all* students are willing to extend themselves. We see anything less than this as failure. However, while we may have high expectations of students, many of them are happy with a 'Pass' grade. For those of us who teach students from low socio-economic backgrounds, a 'Pass' can be a major achievement.

Designing our courses to a set of *core requirements*, complemented by extension activities, can focus our effort on what's important, while still rewarding those who are willing to extend themselves. Our effort should contribute toward student success. We can't do student work for them, but we can help them make sense of information and context.

Students will focus on what is being assessed. If something is critical from our perspective, we must find a way to incorporate it into assessment.

We can spend a lot of time summarising work and spending lectures outlining what we are looking for in assignments, to no avail if no-one is listening. I've already touched on this. As an example, we know that pre-feedback raises the standard of submissions.

Inverting the tornado 85

Pre-feedback explores common errors, specifies problems that may have emerged in previous cohorts, provides exemplars, or works through examples.

Many strategies will improve student performance if students take notice of what we're doing for them. Doing repeat work every term, however, is wasted effort. For example, many of us spend time to develop resources that we host online to explain tasks or concepts. How can we encourage students to engage with those resources that will help them? Examples of how this may be embedded in assessment include:

- 'Watch this video and tell me what you did to ensure these problems/issues did not occur in your experiment/report/submission'.
- 'Read the feedback summary <insert link> and answer the multiple-choice quiz that confirms your knowledge of key points identified'.
- 'Write a 200-word summary at the beginning of your report/essay/presentation that outlines the feedback you received on your draft, and what you did to address this (in point form)'.
- 'A requirement of this assessment piece is that you attend the pre-feedback session to be held on <session details>. If you cannot attend, ensure someone is available to attend in your place. You will be required to discuss, in a 200-word summary, the steps you took to ensure you addressed the issues raised in this session'.
- 'In your reflective blog (assessed), Activity 3 requires you to review the feedback session from last term's course. Write 150 words on how you will avoid similar problems'.

This type of assessment becomes hard to sell to contract cheaters because it's small, requires work, and is personalised. It requires work by us to set up the feedback session, summarise feedback, or create a video, but the hour that this requires in terms of effort will likely save us many. Again, 10 minutes saved in marking because assessments are better quality may save up to 20 hours per marking block if we're marking 120 students, even taking into account those few poorer quality submissions that will still find their way to us and take that extra time to mark.

Adding extra assessments, such as multiple choice quizzes, can be difficult when assessment policies in some institutions restrict the number of assessment pieces (for example, two major summative pieces only with a term). That's why I embed the 'response to feedback' as an assessment requirement *within* existing pieces.

> ***Example of practice:*** *In my advanced feature writing class, I found I was providing consistent feedback about problems I could see in students' reporting work when they were covering scheduled events – lack of accreditation, missing the action, not getting a comment from the organiser. I decided to film a 6-minute video that covered those things that were most important when reporting on a live event – accreditation requirements, reviewing the schedule prior to attendance, and contacting organisers for the appropriate spokesperson. I specifically identified these three key requirements for reporting a live event, and outlined some 'tips and tricks'.*

86 *Inverting the tornado*

The idea was that students would watch the video, reflect on what they needed to do to ensure their reporting would be successful, receive feedback on this, and then report on their event.

It was clear, however, that some students weren't watching the video. Even though I had spent the time to help students, I was still making the same comments on assessment submitted by students who hadn't watched the video.

The following term, I revised assessment to require students to review the video *prior* to reporting on the event. I asked students to identify the three key points I make in the video in an assessable reflective blog. This was submitted and assessed *prior* to students attending and reporting on their event.

That video became the only resource in my course that was watched by all students. From this point, results improved, students felt more confident, and I saved time because I wasn't saying the same thing over and over to students (even if this was a comments bank cut and paste). Win-win.

My strategy was to pre-empt issues in an online video, and require students to watch this, summarise the key points, and incorporate their responses into assessment.

In other courses whereby earlier drafts are reviewed and assessed, I simply require students to submit a journal/justification/response to feedback note with their submission. This raises the likelihood that students will have at least reviewed the initial feedback provided. Here's an example of a 'response to feedback' criteria line in my rubric.

Demonstrated application of feedback					
Criteria element	*Fail*	*Pass*	*Credit*	*Distinction*	*High distinction*
Demonstrated application of feedback.	Limited evidence that feedback provided in class or to earlier stories has been applied, where this was required.	Good evidence that feedback provided in class or to earlier stories has been applied, where this was required.	Evidence that feedback provided in class or to earlier stories has been applied to result in a very good level of improvement to your news writing, where this was required.	Evidence that feedback provided in class or to earlier stories has been applied to result in an excellent level of improvement to your news writing, where this was required.	Evidence that feedback provided in class or to earlier stories has been applied to result in an outstanding level of improvement to your news writing, where this was required.

Future-proof content

We have covered this point before, but it's here as an 'inverting tornado' strategy rather than 'controlling time' strategy because investing time in content, smartly, can increase impact. A common complaint if we don't work smartly is that many online courses include old material – online lectures, outdated readings, links that don't work. It becomes a

Inverting the tornado 87

cycle of doom. We don't have time to create new resources, so we use old ones, and students complain. We must deal with those complaints, and therefore don't have time to create new resources. The following reinforces the differences between simply saving time, and increasing impact for students.

Time thief: As an online teacher, I was unable to reuse previous session online lectures because invariably there was a reference to something current – 'a great example happened this week', 'the current practice is', and so on. It was incredibly frustrating, because 95% of what I was talking about was still current, but I considered the lectures unusable – so, every session, I would redo the lectures.

Controlled time: Driven by the question *'How can I prevent having to redo lectures?'*, I changed my practice. I focused on short concept-based lectures that were future-proofed. If referring to recent practice, I would use the year in objective terms: 'The 2019 Walkley Award-winning feature' rather than 'This year's feature'. This practice saved me 12 hours per term in preparation time routinely. I turned my online lectures into student-focused sessions discussing assessment.

Increased impact: Each time we teach, we are confronted with new information, and interesting, relevant cases emerge. It is important to refresh our teaching materials – we can't rely on the same cases forever, even if they are future-proofed. I ask the question: *'How can I maximise the investment of time I make in embedding this information into my teaching?'*. I embed concept-based lectures or cases into assessment. In some cases, I create them myself. In others, I ask students to build the case or create the example.

Here is an illustrative example:

In December 2018, a large tower in Sydney, Australia, was evacuated due to cracking. The tower (referred to as the Opal Tower) was newly built. It housed thousands of people. This would be a fantastic case to explore from a range of perspectives – engineering, building design, architecture, communication. There are many ways to insert this into our teaching:

1   *deliver an on-campus lecture to class;*
2   *write an overview of the case for in-class discussion;*
3   *develop a video-lecture that explains/discusses the case; or*
4   *ask students to conduct research as a group on the case during class for an end of workshop/tutorial presentation (better still if these types of presentations are assessed).*

One approach that would reduce spin is to spend time developing a case study outline that could be used in tutorials or distributed online, or better still, integrated into assessment. Removing any reference to 'this week' or 'this year' makes the case timeless, noting that cases like this may need to be updated because of post-event investigations and findings (in this case, more examples of unstable apartment buildings emerged in 2019). Seeking support from an instructional designer within

88   *Inverting the tornado*

your institution with the view to make a timeless or update-able case study might be a good investment of time.

Which option would I chose? Option 4 every time, informed by the knowledge that students will learn most by teaching others.

As discussed already, thinking about how our course materials will be viewed or could be used in future terms will streamline our future teaching. This doesn't exonerate us from updating our materials – quite the opposite. We will need to contextualise older videos or cases, but it does mean we build a body of work that we can call on. Especially if we are lucky enough to look after one course over a long period of time.

Finally, some of you will be thinking: *'All that is fine, but the student didn't read the requirement for assessment'*. That's where self-assessment as a requirement helps.

Self-assessment

Self-assessment is a tornado-inverting strategy from a purely pragmatic perspective. Marking student work that is missing aspects of the assignment requirements, or off-track, is a waste of an hour of life I can't get back. I am not an education teacher. Teaching students *how* to self-assess is not a clearly-stated learning outcome associated with my courses. It is therefore not an inherent requirement that I teach my students how to self-assess, nor am I required to assess how they do assess themselves. I simply want students to read the assessment criteria so they know what they need to do. I know it can be complicated, but it can also be simple.

We can simply require students to review the marking rubric and highlight that section of the rubric to which they think their work applies. We don't need to be concerned about the quality of the self-assessment, as it should always be our intention to review the assignment. We simply want to read an assignment and know that the student has, as a minimum, reviewed the requirements of the assignment and made an attempt to engage with the topic.

Very simply, employing self-assessment drives students to reflect on their own practices.

Personal reflection: After implementing self-assessment, I was surprised by the results. Students, initially nervous about what I was looking for, relaxed when I explained that they were not assessed on 'how' they assessed themselves. I include a short video-based example as instructions to students, and explain that they are simply required to 'have a go' at reviewing their work. Importantly, it is a requirement and one of my rubric lines is 'Attention to the requirements of the task' – one of those requirements being to complete the rubric themselves. Students include the self-assessed rubric with their assignments, always within the one file so I don't have to open multiple files (which wastes time).

Many are very candid. I receive comments within the self-assessed rubrics such as: 'I worked really hard, and hope I did well' to 'I am disappointed in my own effort this term, but had to juggle a few issues. I will try harder next time'. Most students are quite accurate in their assessment, but some are not – they either over-estimate their ability or clearly lack confidence.

This allows me to have a conversation with students. I can build up those who have under-estimated their results, or be very careful about the feedback to those who have a highly inflated sense of self.

Some people assess students on that student's ability to assess their own performance. This is perfectly reasonable if your students are completing teaching, assessing, or coaching courses, but in my courses, it would mean I would need to teach students *how* to self-assess. I don't want to overcomplicate matters – I simply want students to be more careful when completing their assignments. An example of an instructive paragraph in my assessment outline is:

> You will be required to complete a self-assessment for this assignment. You are required to complete the marking criteria as if you were marking the assignment and give yourself a grade. Include this with your assignment with an overall summary statement. Why do we ask you to do this? We know that requiring you to self-assess encourages you to engage with assessment requirements more deeply, and therefore gives you a better chance of achieving a higher grade. Your work will be marked independently, and you will be given feedback about your self-assessment.

Students who become used to self-assessment will ask for it. I love being able to say things like: 'I noted that you graded yourself X. You are really talented and can be more confident that you are on the right track', or alternatively, 'I noted that you graded yourself a little higher than my assessment. I acknowledge the clear evidence of hard work, but would encourage you to engage more directly with X. . . . You will see great improvement if you do Y'. I haven't had a formal or informal review of grade on any of my grading since I implemented self-assessment (thousands of students), which is complemented by personalised feedback.

Chapter 6 summary and activity

This chapter has discussed collective strategies that can maximise the impact of effort with the view to encourage students to engage with our efforts to assist them. The next chapter reviews some of the literature on some suggested strategies as a little bit of confirmation and support for anyone nervous about some of the ideas presented so far.

Chapter 6 activity – invert your tornado

Identify three things you could do that collectively might have greater impact on your time and student success. Support this with some baseline statistics or reflections:

'I teach a course called X. There are X number of students enrolled each term. (comment on issues/demographics/challenges)'.

90 *Inverting the tornado*

'Overall, the student pass rate is X. Student satisfaction rates are X (include information here that builds a holistic picture of "student success")'.

'My current practice is X (outline current practice – assessment, communication, attitude)'.

'I am going to change these three things: (outline your focus). I will do this by: (outline timeline and approach – e.g. progressively, over three sessions, next time I take a class)'.

This can become a baseline claim for a teaching award/promotion/tenure/paper. When we are successful, we will have recorded the start point from which we can demonstrate a positive impact on student learning. We will have time to write this because we will have saved ourselves some hours!

References and further reading

You can read more about my 'experiment' with discovery learning in an online environment here:

Ames, K. (2016). Distance education and 'discovery learning' in first-year journalism: A case in subject improvement. *Asia Pacific Media Educator, 26*(2), 214–225. doi:10.1177/1326365X16669196

You can read about my reflection on student video watching here:

Ames, K. (2014, October 23). *Using video in distance education teaching materials*. Blog. Retrieved from https://onlineedreflections.wordpress.com/2014/10/23/using-video-in-distance-education-teaching-materials/

Subsequent to this post, I stopped recording weekly lectures (saving 24 hours per term) for that particular course, which was writing-based and devoted the time to personally calling students (which took me the equivalent 24 hours per term approximately). Only three in ten students (roughly) answered the calls, but all students knew I had tried to contact them. Satisfaction and pass scores improved in relevant offerings. It was a better use of the time I had available.

7 How do we know it works?

If you're still here, there's a chance you're committed to change, but still a bit nervous. This may especially be the case if you are a balanced or research-based academic, and perhaps lack some of the educational knowledge a teaching-focused scholar may have. This very short chapter aims to provide a little bit of evidence in the face of doubt. It focuses on those aspects of practice that I have found most difficult to 'convince' others will work. These are setting boundaries in the form of virtual contact hours, self-assessment, and peer review.

Setting boundaries

Many academics are nervous about setting boundaries if they are willing supporters of students. There isn't much known within academic contexts about how students feel about time-based office hours; most of the attention has been paid to personal/professional relationships (see Chory & Offstein, 2017; Hosek & Thompson, 2009). Known exceptions are the studies following.

In 2009, Lei Li and Jennifer Pitts from Columbus State University examined the impact of online or virtual contact hours in addition to face-to-face or on-campus contact hours. They found that students in classes that offered virtual contact hours were more satisfied than students in classes that offered only traditional face-to-face consultation hours. They valued the ability to contact teaching staff without having to come to class.

In 2013, Mario Guerrero and Alisa Rod investigated the correlation between office hours and academic performance, noting that a student's attendance during contact hours reflected positively on their performance. This is supported by others such as McGrath (2013), who also linked office hour attendance with better student performance. This mirrors, in a way, results from learning analytic work in online courses that highlight the link between engagement with an online course and learning success – that is, the more you engage with the course, the better students perform (Beer & Lawson, 2016).

92 *How do we know it works?*

'Starting the Conversation: An Exploratory Study of Factors That Influence Student Office Hour Use' (Griffen et al., 2014) provides a useful overview as to the factors that influence office hour use. Students were more likely to attend office hours if online discussion was perceived as not useful, if instructor feedback was perceived as useful, and if location and time of office hours were suitable. More recently, Briody, Wirtz, Goldenstein, and Berger (2019) studied faculty-student interaction to identify factors influencing student interaction with faculty.

The recommendation from these studies is that academics *invest more heavily in the contact hour process* to promote student success. This is completely counter to my premise, which is that students should want and need less of our individual time during contact or office hours. The premise that we should be encouraging students to seek our personal attention in office hours as an example of good practice is quite flawed. If we implement strategies such as phone calls, audio feedback, and responses and recognition on discussion forums by name during virtual contact hours, as examples, we provide the faculty interaction students are seeking in potentially more meaningful ways than waiting for students to come to us with a specific question.

We want our students to be able to work independently and understand requirements without seeking further clarification. For online teachers, this is particularly important, and noted by assessment 'guru' David Boud when he reflected on having to change his practice when he started teaching distance students in the 1980s: "Teaching through paper and tape provided a discipline which forced me to be much more explicit and unambiguous about what was involved than I had been previously" (2013, p. 7).

The more students contact me for clarification or personal feedback, the more questions I have about what is possibly wrong with my course design. We need to question why students seek interaction with faculty outside of class. If we can provide useful instructor feedback in other ways, manage online discussion so that it is useful, and establish virtual office hours to communicate with students (online or face to face) in a contained and orderly way, as examples, then it is likely that fewer students will feel the need to contact me personally.

I have yet to do specific research on my approach, but course satisfaction scores for my distance classes follow. The average scores for my institution are indicated by (*) - the reason I share this is that as I changed my practice (which included becoming much stricter with student contact), satisfaction of students increased. The numbers in parentheses are student response rates and number of distance students in the course (noting that in many terms I was also teaching on-campus students). By 2017-2018, I was using audio feedback, peer review, FAQs, strict contact hours, self- and peer assessment, detailed rubrics, and personal phone calls, and had ceased formal lectures because no-one turned up. My High Distinction rate in Feature Writing in 2018 was above 50%, with many articles published in real publications (the results were so high I sought external moderation to ensure I wasn't being too easy in my marking). I was teaching while in a managerial role, and enjoying both.

How do we know it works? 93

Example of increased satisfaction rates

Course	2013 (3.9*)	2014 (4.0*)	2015 (4.1*)	2016 (4.1*)	2017 (4.2*)	2018 (4.2*)
First year						
Media Writing	N/A	4.2 (49%/73)	4.3 (43%/84)	4.3 (41%/104)	4.6 (47%/46)	N/A
Intro Journ	4.3 (39%/28)	3.7 (56%/16)	4.6 (52%/29)	N/A	N/A	N/A
Second year						
News Writing	N/A	4.1 (54%/13)	5.0 (33%/3)	N/A	4.7 (62%/22)	N/A
Feature Writing	4.6 (36%/25)	4.8 (50%/12)	N/A	4.7 (61%/36)	N/A	4.8 (41%/29)
Third year						
Speech & Script	N/A	4.5 (53%/32)	N/A	4.8 (52%/42)	N/A	4.9 (41%/44)
Comm Project	4.0 (50%/2)	4.7 (39%/18)	4.6 (60%/35)	4.5 (60%/10)	4.9 (62%/13)	N/A

Feedback

The way we provide feedback to students affects our time. There is so much written on this that I won't labour any points, but my practice models the 'assessment for learning' approach as opposed to 'assessment as a test'. Sambell, Brown, and Graham (2017) provide some excellent summaries and examples of practice, and if you are completely new to the concept, the Australian website www.assessmentforlearning.edu.au provides some excellent introductory information, which is targeted at K-12 teachers but is also relevant to higher education educators. This means that feedback is critical, constructive, and focuses on longer-term outcomes such as improving a student's ability to self-evaluate (Boud & Molloy, 2013, p. 15).

Feedback is not simple, or easy to deliver. It is one of the most problematic areas for students and for staff who may be completely new to writing and assessing student work against a particular 'standard'. Royce Sadler's work on developing assessment standards is important if you are new to writing assessment criteria or developing rubrics (as examples of many, see Sadler, 1983, 2005, 2009).

The manner in which we provide feedback to students can have a bigger impact than that moment in which we give feedback. Simple tick/pass responses, or lack of detail or constructive comment, can have consequences. Those in senior roles will know that key areas of complaint relate to the way in which feedback is delivered to students. If you find you are spending time handling student complaints about feedback, then it is worth investing some time into developing effective feedback strategies that go beyond the wording of comments or the way in which rubrics are constructed (although these are important). In addition to Royce Sadler, my go-to scholars in this area generally include Phil Race (see https://phil-race.co.uk/), Sally Brown (https://sally-brown.net), David Carless (https://davidcarless.edu.hku.hk/), and David Boud.

Self-assessment

Why don't more of us incorporate self-assessment into our practice? I would be a rich woman for every discussion I have had with peers about this. Arguments against it range from: 'Students aren't expert enough to self-assess their performance' to 'I don't want

94 *How do we know it works?*

to overcomplicate things'. Self-assessment encourages learners to make judgements about their achievements against learning outcomes, increases their role as active participants in their own learning, and often is used formatively to foster reflection on learning (Boud, 2013). In very simple terms, it requires students to identify standards/criteria that apply to their work and make judgements about the 'extent to which they have met these criteria and standards' (Boud, in Liu & Carless, 2006, p. 281).

Broader knowledge about self-assessment has identified, as examples:

- Good students tend to underrate, and weaker students overrate, themselves (Boud & Falchikov, 1989).
- More advanced students were better at self-assessment than lower level students, and the ability for students to self-assess accurately improves over time (Boud & Falchikov, 1989).
- Students interpret self-assessment tasks contextually (Dochy, Segers, & Sluijsmans, 1999).
- Overall, students are more accurate than not at grading their own work, but weaker students have greater difficulty understanding individual criteria (Dochy et al., 1999).
- Those who participate in self-assessment while learning will perform better than those who complete assessment without self-assessment, despite variation in self-assessment methods (Dochy et al., 1999).
- Self-assessment has been shown to increase student understanding of the relationship between content, context, and ability (Dochy et al., 1999).
- Students are reliable assessors generally (Liu & Carless, 2006).

In short, self-assessment improves student performance, ability to reflect on practice, and understanding over time. Most importantly for us, it makes our life easier because students perform better, take responsibility for their learning, and as a minimum, read the criteria and seek early clarification of requirements.

Reviewing the different methods of self-assessment promulgated in the literature, it becomes clear that there's no one method. There's a strong argument for teaching students about self-assessment and reflection, and embedding this in a broader course delivery framework. However, this book is targeted at individual academics trying to make things easier while increasing the quality of work by our students. There's not much I can add to David Boud's comprehensive book, *Enhancing Learning through Self-Assessment* (2013), which I highly recommend to anyone considering student self-assessment.

Peer review

Peer review can occur in the form of feedback or assessment. Liu and Carless note the distinction: Peer feedback requires students to engage with performance and standards associated with assessment, while peer assessment requires students to grade students using relevant criteria (2006). I don't practice peer assessment; I prefer self-assessment,

How do we know it works? 95

for a range of reasons well covered in the literature, but I do encourage peer feedback and incorporate this into assessment.

The value in peer review is because the simple act of giving feedback is as important as receiving it (Dominick, Reilly, & McGourty, 1997; Nicol, Thomson, & Breslin, 2014), and students don't have to receive feedback (they simply need to give it) to improve their performance (Dominick et al., 1997). Like self-assessment, peer review requires students to engage with assessment criteria. Overall, we know that peer review:

- helps improve student performance (see Dominick et al., 1997);
- shifts students from passive learners to active participants (McGourty, Dominick, & Reilly, 1998; Nicol & Macfarlane-Dick, 2006);
- reinforces key learning objectives (McGourty et al., 1998);
- reinforces the message that student work can be improved;
- is acknowledged by students to be effective (Burke Moneypenny, Evans, & Kraha, 2018); and
- needs to be contextualised, particularly with regard to differences between online and face-to-face delivery (Burke Moneypenny et al., 2018).

In my case, developing a policy of public drafting in addition to peer review reduced questions and provided students with evidence of what I was looking for. I have referred previously to my approach to public drafting, whereby students send me a draft prior to class. I work through their drafts in class, publicly – online students submit assessment drafts to me via the discussion forum for peer and teacher feedback. Most students won't, but some do – often high achievers, but not all. There appears to be a flow on effect in that students take notice of the feedback I provide to others. Of course, there needs to be recognition as to why students don't participate – Kelly Rocca's 2010 meta-analysis of research into student participation in the classroom provides a useful overview.

Overall, there are many decades of research into peer review and assessment, but changes in the way education is delivered provides new challenges as to how they can be adopted in the classroom. Academics are reluctant to engage in peer feedback or peer assessment for many reasons (Liu & Carless, 2006), but the evidence is in favour of peer review in particular.

Chapter 7 summary and activity

This chapter has emphasised that there is a body of knowledge that supports setting boundaries, and feedback strategies such as self-assessment and peer review. It is worth familiarising yourself with some of this knowledge, seeking support from a mentor to help you implement some of the strategies, and view any changes in practice as opportunities for scholarship. Remember that we're working toward improving the quality of student work, and their knowledge of what is required of them. If we are successful in this, the hours we spend setting up tasks and providing instruction or guidance will pay off by saving us time in the longer term.

Note that the list of references below barely scratches the surface of what is available!

96 *How do we know it works?*

Chapter 7 activity – reading

Select one reading from the list below. I recommend Sambell et al. (2017) as a starting text. Record any ideas you may have that emerge from this reading.

Identify one element of practice you might change the next time you teach.

References

Beer, C., & Lawson, C. (2016). The problem of student attrition in higher education: An alternative perspective. *Journal of Further and Higher Education*, 1–12. doi:10.1080/0309877X.2016.1177171

Boud, D. (2013). *Enhancing learning through self-assessment*. London: Routledge.

Boud, D., & Falchikov, N. (1989). Quantitative studies of student self-assessment in higher education: A critical analysis of findings. *Higher Education, 18*(5), 529–549. doi:10.1007/bf00138746

Boud, D., & Molloy, E. (2013). Changing conceptions of feedback. In D. Boud & E. Molloy (Eds.), *Feedback in higher and professional education* (pp. 11–33). London: Routledge.

Briody, E. K., Wirtz, E., Goldenstein, A., & Berger, E. J. (2019). Breaking the tyranny of office hours: Overcoming professor avoidance. *European Journal of Engineering Education*, 1–22. doi:10.1080/03043797.2019.1592116

Burke Moneypenny, D., Evans, M., & Kraha, A. (2018). Student perceptions of and attitudes toward peer review. *American Journal of Distance Education, 32*(4), 236–247. doi:10.1080/08923647.2018.1509425

Chory, R. M., & Offstein, E. H. (2017). "Your professor will know you as a person" evaluating and rethinking the relational boundaries between faculty and students. *Journal of Management Education, 41*(1), 9–38. doi:10.5465/ambpp.2016.10176abstract

Dochy, F., Segers, M., & Sluijsmans, D. (1999). The use of self-, peer and co-assessment in higher education: A review. *Studies in Higher Education, 24*(3), 331–350. doi:10.1080/03075079912331379935

Dominick, P. G., Reilly, R. R., & McGourty, J. W. (1997). The effects of peer feedback on team member behavior. *Group & Organization Management, 22*(4), 508–520. doi:10.1177/1059601197224006

Griffen, W., Cohen, S. D., Berndtson, R., Burson, K. M., Camper, K. M., Chen, Y., & Smith, M. A. (2014). Starting the conversation: An exploratory study of factors that influence student office hour use. *College Teaching, 62*(3), 94–99. doi:10.1080/87567555.2014.896777

Guerrero, M., & Rod, A. B. (2013). Engaging in office hours: A study of student-faculty interaction and academic performance. *Journal of Political Science Education, 9*(4), 403–416. doi:10.1080/15512169.2013.835554

Hosek, A. M., & Thompson, J. (2009). Communication privacy management and college instruction: Exploring the rules and boundaries that frame instructor private disclosures. *Communication Education, 58*(3), 327–349. doi:10.1080/03634520902777585

Li, L., & Pitts, J. P. (2009). Does it really matter? Using virtual office hours to enhance student-faculty interaction. *Journal of Information Systems Education, 20*(2), 175–185.

Liu, N. F., & Carless, D. (2006). Peer feedback: The learning element of peer assessment. *Teaching in Higher Education, 11*(3), 279–290. doi:10.1080/13562510600680582

McGourty, J., Dominick, P., & Reilly, R. R. (1998). *Incorporating student peer review and feedback into the assessment process*. Paper presented at the FIE 28th Annual Frontiers in Education Washington, DC, November 4–7. doi:10.1109/fie.1998.736790

McGrath, A. L. (2013). Just checking in: The effect of an office hour meeting and learning reflection in an introductory statistics course. *Teaching of Psychology, 41*(1), 83–87. doi:10.1177/0098628313514186

Nicol, D. J., & Macfarlane-Dick, D. (2006). Formative assessment and self-regulated learning: A model and seven principles of good feedback practice. *Studies in Higher Education, 31*(2), 199–218. doi:10.1080/03075070600572090

Nicol, D. J., Thomson, A., & Breslin, C. (2014). Rethinking feedback practices in higher education: A peer review perspective. *Assessment & Evaluation in Higher Education, 39*(1), 102–122. doi:10.1080/02602938.2013.795518

How do we know it works? 97

Rocca, K. A. (2010). Student participation in the college classroom: An extended multidisciplinary literature review. *Communication Education, 59*(2), 185-213. doi:10.1080/03634520903505936

Sadler, D. R. (1983). Evaluation and the improvement of academic learning. *The Journal of Higher Education, 54*(1), 60-79. doi:10.2307/1981645

Sadler, D. R. (2005). Interpretations of criteria-based assessment and grading in higher education. *Assessment & Evaluation in Higher Education, 30*(2), 175-194. doi:10.1080/02602930400026426 2

Sadler, D. R. (2009). Indeterminacy in the use of preset criteria for assessment and grading. *Assessment & Evaluation in Higher Education, 34*(2), 159-179. doi:10.1080/02602930801956059

Sambell, K., Brown, S., & Graham, L. (2017). Engaging students with positive learning experiences through assessment and feedback. In *Professionalism in Practice* (pp. 139-187). London: Springer. doi:10.1007/978-3-319-54552-3_5

8 Tornado-proofing for academics

As we draw to the end of this book, I'll confess to the difficulty with writing it. If you follow me on Twitter, you would have noticed my occasional tweets about writer's block and revision. I am a writer by trade, but in this case feel very exposed. Despite being recognised for my teaching practice through awards and consistent excellent results in a pretty complex teaching institution, I still asked myself: *'Who am I to be writing this? Why is my practice better? Who knows my practice works?'*. But I was reminded, again and again, by peers, mentees, and reading widely, that I had something to contribute.

If only one person reading this gets some part of their life back, even an hour or two a week so they can make progress on an article they are writing, that's great.

Everyone is different when it comes to making changes. Some people will mark a line in the sand and state: *'From this point, I am going to do things differently'*. Others will take a more incremental approach, as I did. I'm not perfect, and I still often take on too much. I sometimes fail, get overwhelmed, and feel like everything has fallen in a heap. As someone who juggles a lot of balls, I find I am at particular risk if I am unwell. It doesn't happen often, but a bout of pneumonia a year or so ago reminded me of how quickly all the planes can crash if you don't pay them regular attention and are unrealistic about your capability.

Ultimately, it will be your choice as to which approach you take.

This chapter summarises the strategies that we have covered as ways to either control the treadmill or invert the tornado. In all, there are 17:

1 Be constructive, kind, polite, respectful, always
2 Create a fixed schedule
3 Establish regular meeting times with research students
4 Take notice of feedback
5 Review/change our thinking
6 Set rules for engagement
7 Create a predictable information cycle for online students
8 Be more effective in our feedback
9 Revise assessment design
10 Build and maintain great teaching teams

Tornado-proofing for academics 99

11 Future-proof course design
12 Become expert in our most commonly used technology
13 Use templates to avoid starting from scratch
14 Schedule social media use
15 Be willing to learn new things
16 Pick up the phone
17 Take a holistic approach

I have listed strategies in order of how I might implement them incrementally. For example, it's easy and simple to start being nice today.

You can take your pick as to which you're going to implement – if any. By this stage, some of this may feel a little repetitive. However, repetition is one of the elements of good teaching practice. It's particularly effective when engaging with new concepts.

Strategy 1 – be constructive, kind, polite, respectful, always

The most immediate step you can take is to change your language if you have identified that you have communication issues. Address students by name when you can, top and tail emails, and avoid being rude. It may take an extra minute at the time you're responding to an email (in virtual office hours only), but the impact goes beyond that moment.

Strategy 2 – create a fixed schedule

You should have identified your fixed schedule in Chapter 3. Review your calendar and start to fix your schedule – regular meetings for PhD students, regular 30-minute meetings for research projects so you can quickly update one another and move on, blocks of time for writing (start with the first 30 minutes of a day, or 30 minutes for lunch), a 3-hour block a month for reviewing a journal article, and so on. Identify the reality of your availability. The next time someone requests something of you, you can see your windows of opportunity – if that window isn't there, you can say, 'Sorry, these few weeks are particularly busy, but I am good after the end of the month'.

Strategy 3 – establish regular meeting times with research students

Research supervision is intense. It's supposed to be guided independent study. As a student, I was able to contact my supervisor when I had questions and needed feedback on writing, but I didn't receive that feedback quickly. My supervision team changed halfway into my study, and one of my new supervisors set regular meetings, with associated tasks. Every fourth Tuesday afternoon was our feedback session. No more email traffic trying to find a time, no more 'have you read my stuff?' questions – simple. The only time we re-arranged was if one of us was travelling.

100   *Tornado-proofing for academics*

As I have discussed in previous chapters, I schedule fortnightly meetings with my students and set small tasks for discussion at each meeting. I spend Monday mornings reviewing any required work. We always meet, even if for 10 minutes just for a quick update. This investment of time prevents issues from emerging, and saves time in the longer term. If we can't fit this time into our schedule, we should question whether we should take on another student.

Strategy 4 - take notice of feedback

We can't know where we need to improve our practice unless we seek feedback. This is tough. When we receive our student evaluations on teaching, we might be defensive and resistant, being keen to blame others. Asking someone else for some objective help to work through areas to address can be useful. They may help you identify those clearly personal comments by a disgruntled student (there's always one who hates you), and those for which you have no influence (such as timetabling). But if you are always returning assignments late, you're always late to class, or if students complain that you never respond to their emails - it's time to come up with a plan to address these points. Not all at once, but make a list. Ask for peer review of your teaching. All of this can contribute to your baseline measure to which you can refer when you apply for your teaching award or promotion.

Strategy 5 - review/change our thinking

Reflect on some of the comments and notes you have made about your practice as you have worked through this book. If you have found yourself in a vortex of negativity, try some cognitive approaches that focus on what's great about your current status. If you're an overworked PhD, you're one of only a few people who made it into a PhD programme; if you're a casual academic juggling multiple balls, you're at least on the radar (many people aren't, because they aren't appropriately qualified). If you don't like students and just want to do your research, reframe your thinking and language - students are future researchers, and if we're supported by public funds, then it's generally within our mission to pay knowledge forward.

Strategy 6 - set rules for engagement

Write a list of rules or principles for your class that provide guidelines for communication. Explain that you are not available after class routinely because you have other commitments, but will be available during virtual and face-to-face office hours (which should be at the same time). Explain that you will maintain a FAQs page on your learning management system that will be updated with responses. Explain that you are supportive and committed to student success, but expect them to take responsibility for their learning journey.

Strategy 7 - create a predictable information cycle for online students

Students have multiple channels available for them to receive communication about their study. Decide how you are going to communicate with students, and minimise the traffic. Expect that students won't come to class unless assessment is tied to activities conducted within class. Perhaps you will email students on Monday mornings with all relevant information associated with class in a week. Alternatively, you might email students on Friday with a summary of the main concepts you need them to have considered that week. If you are making changes to assessment or timetables (which are triggers for complaint cancer), make decisions early and communicate via that one channel. Ensure that online and on-campus students are receiving the same information. If you work with a team of tutors, discuss ways to ensure everyone is on the same page. I do not make any changes once a term has started. I ensure that all extra sessions (such as guest lectures and online drop-in sessions) are scheduled before term starts so students can plan, and post a weekly message every Monday morning.

Strategy 8 - be more effective in our feedback

Effective feedback doesn't need to be time-consuming (although it will take more time than a tick for a pass assignment, and a number on the side of a paper). The benefit of investing in feedback is that if done smartly, and scaffolded so that students are required to address it within the parameters of their assessment, it will result in better quality work. This will be quicker (and more interesting) to mark. Personalised feedback, peer review, peer assessment, and self-assessment are feedback-related strategies that can make a positive difference to student learning and reduce the amount of time you devote to marking.

Strategy 9 - revise assessment design

Review your assessment design to identify ways in which feedback strategies can be embedded. If our courses rely on right/wrong answers, consider the relationship between formative assessment (such as a pass/fail online quiz that tests basic knowledge) and summative assessment that is more engaging. Academics often balk at this because 'engaging' can mean 'complicated' - but when we actually measure the hours we spend orienting students and supporting them in initial stages compared to traditional approaches, we can be surprised at how much time we can save.

Strategy 10 - build and maintain great teaching teams

If you're a member of a teaching team, be proactive in considering yourself part of a bigger team and ask for what you need. Assume you'll be working with this course again, and file/organise so that you can reuse or repurpose information. If you are a course convenor,

102 *Tornado-proofing for academics*

communicate regularly with your teaching team, and like PhD students, schedule regular meetings into the calendar early. Strategies such as social moderation and exemplar explanation can ensure everyone is on the same page. Inconsistent marking and teaching approach generate student complaints – assume they will *always* talk to one another. Most importantly, teaching team members who are willing to work together, familiar with course material, and familiar to students, are more valuable than we can imagine.

Strategy 11 – future-proof course design

Think about how this lecture/video will look in three years' time. Avoid incorporating information that will easily date online materials – page numbers in textbooks (refer to sections or chapters), or references to 'this term', 'this year', or 'this week'. Web-based links are quite stable these days, but I often use Wakelet to manage links in my online courses. As an example, I will refer to my Wakelet storyboard rather than list individual links in those courses I teach that require me to reference current stories. This isn't an excuse to ignore the requirement to update materials. It just means that the review of course material prior to a term might take half a day as opposed to a week.

Strategy 12 – become expert in our most commonly used technology

If the only tools you use to teach are Microsoft Word, Excel, and PowerPoint, and Adobe Acrobat/Reader, become an expert in these. Most of us use only minimum functionality when these products are extremely sophisticated, integrated, and actually easy to use. Features like 'Speak' or 'Read Aloud' in Word that reads writing aloud, being able to email directly from final proofs, merge/compare documents, and merge to PDF – these are huge savers of time. Anyone who has lost more than half an hour to formatting quirks in Microsoft Word should consider some lunchtime YouTube tutorials useful.

Strategy 13 – use templates to avoid starting from scratch

Anything you need to do more than once should be templated. Ethics applications (justifications for methodology), weekly messages to students ('Welcome to Week 1. This week we are exploring . . .', 'By the end of this week, you should have . . .'), feedback rubrics, comment banks for marking, guidelines for tutors, engagement rules for the term, course housekeeping, etc. There is quite a long list. Work on a filing system so that you can easily call for the required template. Issues can arise when due care isn't taken in completing these – cut and paste errors trigger complaint cancer. A template might only save you 15 minutes at a time, but that adds up to big savings overall.

Strategy 14 – schedule social media use

I use social media to engage with students and peers. I limit its use to those times when it's not productive to be doing something else; waiting for an online meeting to start, waiting for the bus, or sitting in the car waiting for a child to finish sport practice. I spend no more than 10 minutes a day on social media, usually Twitter and LinkedIn. This amounts to almost an hour a week. Over a year, that's a little more than a week of time. I consider this a good investment – akin to the time I would spend doing literature reviews, as many of my connections are also academics and promote their latest research via social media.

Simply have a plan for social media use. Unlike many productivity experts who recommend we don't use social media, we're academics. We should be promulgating knowledge and sharing ideas, and the public sphere is bigger than corporately owned journals. Just don't spend all day getting distracted. One hour a day amounts to 5 hours a week. That's 260 hours a year, which is six and a half weeks' worth of work. You could do a lot of other things in that equivalent time.

Strategy 15 – be willing to learn new things

We are often unwilling to be open to learning new things given that we're usually in 'new thing overload'. New learning management systems, new technology, new software, as examples. We become very comfortable with what we know. I am an early adopter of technology because I have taught distance education since the mid-1990s as a media educator. Platforms like iSpring (which converts PowerPoint to online learning packages), Wakelet (which allows me to curate and narrate online content and share publicly), Evernote (for personal management), Trello (for project management), Microsoft Teams (for research project communication), Google Drive (for collaborative writing), and Scrivener (for writing) are now in my daily toolbox. These have become those tools I use most, so I have learned to become expert in them. I am still willing to try new things, but usually when they are shown to me by a respected peer. I will then weigh up whether the time investment in learning the platform is worth it. I am so committed to the benefit of EndNote (or Mendeley/Zotero, whichever you may use) in saving time, for example, that I won't co-write with other scholars unless they are willing to commit to learning how to use a reference management tool. Be open to peer review by staff or for others. It can be enlightening as to how others do things.

Strategy 16 – pick up the phone

Be willing to pick up the phone to talk to students. This creates connection, builds relationships, and can prevent bigger issues emerging. If you're uncomfortable with phone conversations (I was when I started), create a script to start the conversation, and note key points you would like to address. In classes below 60, I call all students once a term. I have a starting script: 'I'm just contacting you to see how you're going, and address any issues you may have . . .'. In most cases, calls go to voicemail. Out of those 60 students, I'll probably talk to 15 directly. Some will call back. I do this because I have clawed back time and now invest hours per term to personal contact as opposed to delivering lectures to which no-one turned up. I could be researching, but I do that too.

104   *Tornado-proofing for academics*

Strategy 17 – take a holistic approach

It's not enough to simply be nice. Many of us are in the predicament we are in because we are too accommodating. It's not enough to simply implement virtual office hours. Asking students to communicate with you only during office hours won't be received well if you're rude the rest of the time. It's not effective to ask students to self-assess if you are finding yourself responding to multiple emails from hundreds of students because you don't have a broader communication or engagement strategy, or approach to FAQs. It's important to have a broader plan.

An example of how things might be different

In Chapter 4, we met many academics struggling to control time. One of our unhappiest was Leah. To recap, this was Leah's story:

> *Leah coordinates a course in introductory creative writing. She has too much assessment, and is marking from Week 3. Students aren't taking notice of feedback, and Leah is struggling to complete her marking on time. Students are complaining, and Leah feels like a personal tutor to some. Many students don't appear committed to the class, and her grading system seems to have promoted the possibility of error in calculation. Leah hates her work. She has no time to herself or her own writing.*

By adopting some of the strategies outlined in this book, Leah can change her story.

> *Leah decides to review her approach with the support of a mentor, so that students are more engaged in feedback. She identifies her fixed schedule, establishes virtual office hours, and schedules review and service periods into her week. She has realised she needs to refine her practice to reduce her marking time and contain her teaching to 16 hours per week in non-marking weeks. She communicates with all students via a weekly forum post distributed on her learning management system on Monday mornings, makes some exemplars available (supported by explanatory video), and establishes an FAQ page for students.*
>
> *Her assessment redesign incorporates peer review, self-assessment, and personalised feedback. She has decided to incorporate an early 'Ideas pitch' session that is compulsory, but has no marks attached, so she can gauge the quality of ideas early. Students simply need to submit four slides outlining their ideas against a set of key questions, and be able discuss their approach to pass.*
>
> *Leah's assessment schedule for her creative writing course looks like this:*

> - *Ideas pitch Week 3 – Pass/Fail*
> - *Peer review Week 4 and Week 10 – Required tasks for Assignments 1 and 2*
> - *Assignment 1 (Creative Piece 1), Due Week 6 – 40%*
> - *Assignment 2 (Creative Piece 2), Due Week 12 – 60%*

Tornado-proofing for academics 105

The class starts with 105 students. Idea pitches occur in class or via online sessions in Week 3, to which students must attend. Those who can't attend are required to book an individual session. Overall, Leah's extra commitment is 4 hours in Week 3 for online sessions and two 15-minute private sessions for students who couldn't make class (4.5 hours overall for the week).

Leah notes that some students have dropped out, realising that this wasn't going to be an 'easy' elective. She reminds students that professional creative writing is a public endeavour, and that giving and receiving feedback are important skills for creative writers. Students are therefore expected to provide feedback on other students' writing. Leah has allocated students into peer review pairs, based on the Think-Pair-Share model. Requirements of the main assignment tasks (Assignments 1 and 2) are that students provide copies of their feedback to other students, and a response to the feedback they were provided: 'I provided feedback to Student A, as evidenced by . . .'; 'Student X provided feedback on my draft. Student X suggested I do X. I responded by . . .'. Leah has developed a short 5-minute video and a two-page guide on how to provide effective feedback for creative writers that are available on her Moodle site, and guidelines for self-assessment. This took her 5 hours to complete.

Leah has a clear communication and engagement policy that requires students to check her FAQ page first before asking questions in class or on the discussion forum. She has invited students to post examples of writing to her online 'Drafts' forum. Some students take this up, and she provides general feedback during her virtual office hours. In Week 4, she provides public feedback on five student submissions, which took 2 hours. She is able to complete this within her virtual office hour time.

Leah starts marking at the end of Week 6. It is clear most students (not all) have engaged with the requirement to peer review someone else's work, and most have responded to the feedback. Some students have not, or clearly left their review to the last minute (around 15 of her 98 remaining students), and some students have failed to self-assess their work. These students fail the requirements of the task, even if they have produced outstanding work. It becomes clear to these students that they will need to engage with their peers for the next round of drafting and self-assess their work. Overall, Leah spends 35 hours marking in Weeks 7 and 8. She uses audio feedback, which cuts down her marking time. Her rubric comments are still basic, but she expands on these as she talks through her response in five-minute recordings.

The same process occurs in Week 10 (peer drafting). Again, Leah offers to review some public drafts. She receives a few more submissions, and spends 4 hours in this week providing general public feedback.

Final assignments are due in Week 12. Leah spends 25 hours marking these – it is clear that most students have engaged with feedback. She still provides audio feedback but notes that for most students, her comments only last 2 minutes as opposed to 5. Some student work is still quite poor, but the vast majority have demonstrated improvement.

106 *Tornado-proofing for academics*

> *At the end of term, she receives no requests for reviews of grades. All of her assignments have been returned on time. Two of her students have gained enough confidence to submit their work to publishers. Leah has loved every minute of being at work. She has had time to do her own writing, including research for a journal article, and while some of the work submitted has been quite plain, and some of the efforts by students to conduct peer review have been clearly half-hearted, some students have fully embraced working with one another. Some of the stories submitted have made her laugh out loud, and cry. She enjoys being a full-time creative writing teacher.*

Leah implemented many of the 17 strategies as a holistic approach to change. Not all – she currently doesn't have research students or engage with social media. At least now she has time to think about whether she wants to tweet or supervise a PhD student!

Moving forward

I have deliberately avoided discussing personal management issues associated with time management because there are so many great books devoted to this. Those that influenced my practice in terms of focus, email management, and prioritisation include James Clear's *Atomic Habits* (2018), Cal Newport's *Deep Work* (2016), and *The Productivity Project* by Chris Bailey (2016). I mentally argued with them all. I wished I had Chris Bailey's uncomplicated single life as I was reading his book, felt I wasn't so driven or ambitious as Cal Newport, and wondered if it really was as simple as James Clear proposed.

From an academic productivity perspective, I have previously noted how much I owe to Maria Gardiner and Hugh Kearns' Thinkwell programme (www.ithinkwell.com. au/) with which I have had the great fortune to be exposed. My ability to keep multiple research projects in the air and continue to research while also juggling a managerial role and teaching is only due to Maria's pragmatic advice. Inger Mewburn's 'Thesis Whisperer' blog (https://thesiswhisperer.com/), Tara Brabazon's video logs (www.youtube. com/user/TaraBrabazon), and Tanya Golash-Bhoza's blog on academic work/life balance (http://getalifephd.blogspot.com/) also provide regular inspiration.

As an online educator, I am *always* looking for the 'how can this be done with distance students?' when I am reviewing academic models of practice. To be a better teacher, I've specifically leaned on resources such as David Carless' *How assessment supports learning: Learning-oriented assessment in action* (with Joughin & Liu, 2006) and *Excellence in university assessment: Learning from award-winning practice* (2015), David Boud's *Enhancing learning through self-assessment* (2016), Phil Race's *The lecturer's toolkit* (2013), and Diana Laurillard's *Teaching as a design science* (2012). Stephen Downes' blog is a routine source of new information and grounded perspective on the relationship between technology and education (www.downes.ca/). I also reference Glen Pearsall's *Fast and effective assessment: How to reduce your workload and improve student learning* (2018). While this book targets on-campus high school learners and teachers, the strategies he employs to save time and increase efficiency in teaching can be applied in higher education settings.

I must also acknowledge the important influence of some CQUniversity colleagues with whom I work closely. Specifically, and relevant to some of the ideas in this book, Professor Ken Purnell shared his practice of audio feedback for online students with me many years ago, and Associate Professor Karena Burke shared her practice of online feedback sessions. I adopted these practices to fit my context, but without their willingness to share ideas at the time, I wonder where I would be today. It reminds me about the importance of creating space in our teaching to talk about what we do in enough detail that others can replicate or adapt our ideas.

Ultimately, this book is about more than managing time. It's about being effective with the teaching side of our workload to address 'seep'. Manya Whitaker's article '10 Things No One Told Me About Applying for Tenure' reminds us that regardless of how much we try to do, 'Meeting the standards may not be enough' (2019). If goalposts keep changing, and we feel we are always at the whim of something larger than ourselves, then it's easy to run fast on the treadmill, getting swept up in other people's tornadoes or creating our own.

Academic life is complex, interesting, overwhelming, and diverse. Whether you're a 'newbie' or a 'prepper', or currently a 'rollercoaster', I hope the some of the scenarios in this book have reminded you that you are not alone, and the discussion and strategies give you some ideas or confidence to take action to control the treadmill, and invert a few tornadoes.

I'll look forward to meeting some of you on Twitter (find me @Kate_Ames). Good luck!

References

Bailey, C. (2016). *The productivity project: Accomplishing more by managing your time, attention, and energy.* Toronto: Random House Canada.

Boud, D. (2016). *Enhancing learning through self-assessment.* London: Taylor & Francis Group.

Carless, D. (2015). *Excellence in university assessment: Learning from award-winning practice.* London: Routledge.

Carless, D., Joughin, G., & Liu, N. F. (2006). *How assessment supports learning: Learning-oriented assessment in action* (Vol. 1). Hong Kong: Hong Kong University Press.

Clear, J. (2018). *Atomic habits: An easy and proven way to build good habits and break bad ones.* New York: Penguin.

Laurillard, D. (2012). *Teaching as a design science.* London: Routledge.

Newport, C. (2016). *Deep work: Rules for focused success in a distracted world.* London: Hachette UK.

Pearsall, G. (2018). *Fast and effective assessment: How to reduce your workload and improve student learning.* Alexandria, VA: ASCD.

Race, P. (2013). *The lecturer's toolkit: A practical guide to assessment, learning and teaching.* London: Routledge.

Whitaker, M. (2019, April 28). 10 things no one told me about applying for tenure. *Chronicle of Higher Education (online).* Retrieved from www.chronicle.com/article/10-Things-No-One-Told-Me-About/246187

INDEX

'9-to-5' life 25

academic identity 4; ambi (ambivalent) 6;
   counter-newbie 6; newbie 5; prepper 7;
   project-focused academic 7; research purist
   6; teacher 7
academic time 23
assessment design 53, 101
attitude 75
audio feedback 83

Bailey, Chris 106
Boud, David 93, 106
Brabazon, Tara 106
Brown, Sally 93
Burke, Karena 107
bushfires 71; management 47

calculating hours 28
Carless, David 93, 106
Clear, James 106
communication 63, 78; student 46
complaint cancer 10, 48, 102
conferences 69
contact hours 63, 72-72, 81, 91-92
core requirements 84
counselling 70
curriculum design 49

Downes, Stephen 106

education: as a privilege 16; as a right 16
email 36
EndNote 69, 103

engagement 75
example of practice 85

failure rate 16
FAQs *see* frequently asked questions
fear 19
feedback 93, 99-101
feeling: important 17; needed 17
fixed: costs 24; hours 30; schedule 99
flexibility 26
flexible hours 25
frequently asked questions (FAQs) 62-63, 73,
   81, 84
future-proof content 86-87, 102

Gardiner, Maria 27, 106
Golash-Bhoza, Tanya 17, 34, 106
Google Drive 103

holistic approach 104
hour breakdown 27, 30

ideal schedule 33
illustrative example: difficult students 83;
   future-proof content 86-87; level playing
   fields 31
important 17
independence 15
information cycle, predictable 101
interpretivist 14
iSpring 103

job profile 3
justifications 19

110 *Index*

Kearns, Hugh 106

lack: of confidence 20; of control 19
Laurillard, Diana 106
lecture preparation 51
level playing fields 31

Mendeley 69, 103
Mewburn, Inger 18, 106
Microsoft Teams 103

Newport, Cal 26, 106

organisational culture 16
organisational systems 16-17
organise information 68
over-assess 66
overcommitment 42
overcomplicate 66

Pearsall, Glen 106
peer: assessment 93-94; feedback 93-94;
   review 93-94
performance measures 3
personal: feedback 82; moments 82;
   organisation 35; reflection 88
phone 103
positivist 14
professional casual 8
public drafting 95
Purnell, Ken 107

Race, Phil 93, 106
reduce: amount of marking 64; email 61
rollercoaster 8
rubric: application of feedback 86;
   requirements of the task 67
rules for engagement 99

Sadler, Royce 93
scenario 77; Arun, student communication
   46; Brian (communication 72-73; email
   36-37); Carol, overcommitment 42;

Huiling (lecture preparation 51; teaching
administration 44); Jane (bushfire
management 47-48; communication 72-73;
email 36-37); Jonathon (social media 38;
teaching materials 49-51); Kevin (attitude
76-77; lecture preparation 51-52; teaching
administration 44-45; technology 56-57);
Leah (assessment design 53-55; doing
things differently 104); Suraya, travel 40-41
Scrivener 103
self-assessment 88, 93-94
setting boundaries 91
social media 38, 58, 102
'speak once to a crowd' 80
story 73
support 15
systems 16

taking stock 20
teaching: administration 44; materials 49
technology 56, 58
templates 102
Thinkwell x, 21, 106
time: as budget 24, 34; thieves 35
tornado 11
travel 40
treadmill 9; routine 60; setting own pace 72;
   slow 61
Trello 103

unnecessary travel 69

variable costs 24
virtual engagement *see* contact hours

Wakelet 103
Whitaker, Manya 107
work-life balance 33
workload 2; allocation 2
work seep 25
worldview 21, 75

Zotero 69, 103